To all who are just beginning their campaigns.

To all who continue.

To all who've left the campaigns behind.

There's a first time for everyone.

My First Time

Advertising's Top Creatives
Talk About Their First
Commercial, Ad or Site,
And What They Learned From It

And That All You've Heard
About The Crazy World Of Advertising
Doesn't Even Come Close

By
Phil Growick

Paperback ISBN 9781780921952
ePub ISBN 9781780921969
PDF ISBN 9781780921976

Published in the UK by MX Publishing
335 Princess Park Manor, Royal Drive, London, N11 3GX
www.mxpublishing.com

Cover design by
www.staunch.com

TABLE OF CONTENTS

Introduction

Nobody starts at the top. Nobody.

While some may be born with a silver spoon, no one is born with a Gold Pencil. Or Gold Lion.

And though there are books on how to become a copywriter or art director or craft a portfolio, which are all very important, there hasn't been a book about how the top creative leaders in advertising began.

What really happened to them when they were creating their first commercial, or ad or site? Who did they want to kiss, who did they want to kill? Who did they promise, with every atom in their bodies, to emulate? And because of whom did they swear a blood oath: "If I ever get to be like that guy, please just shoot me?"

All the people whose stories you'll read here had one thing in common: they started at the bottom. Their business cards didn't have an address; they just said: Look down.

There were few, if any, ad schools back then. And like anyone just starting out, they all wanted the chance to show what they could do. Just like you. They just wanted to impress the creative gods who were their ECDs or CCOs. Gods who either mentor or menace.

The top world creatives who tell their stories here are the mentors. The people who are at the peak of the advertising food chain, but who believe there's room at the table for everyone. They just want to have fun and make sure no one goes hungry.

All of their stories are funny, some are very touching or a combination of the two. And some are just too bizarre to believe. But then again, *nothing* in the ad world is too bizarre to believe. Which is what makes it so much fun.

To draw on that funny, quirky, ironic and bizarre world, you'll be reading about leaders still at major agencies, and some who'd been at major agencies but who've struck out to begin their own, hopefully soon-to-be, major agencies.

Now, who am I and how did I come to arrange this creative conclave?

As the cover says, I'm Phil Growick, Managing Director of the Howard-Sloan-Koller Group. In a gentle colloquialism, I'm a headhunter for top world talent. Top talent who are also really top people. And I'm doing it at the best executive search firm in the world (okay, so I'm a bit prejudiced here, but it's true).

It's been my good fortune over the past twenty years or so, to become friends and colleagues with many of the people whose stories are here.

Many I've known since they were considerably more junior and I've watched, or helped, them achieve their goal of becoming some of the top creative people they are today. Some I've never met but have spoken with over the years, always with great enjoyment. And some I contacted specifically to be part of this book because I had heard such great things about them.

In fact, as further flavor, after you read each bio, before each story, I'll give you my thoughts about that person. A behind-the-scenes assessment of their personalities and the kind of people they are. If there isn't a lengthy "My Thoughts" for a particular person, it's only because I haven't known that individual well enough to give you any more info other than this: if they weren't who they were, as creative as they were, and with a valuable story to tell, they wouldn't be in this book.

Name the award, the people in this book have won it. Numerous times. But the one thing all these people have in common, which is why our relationship has remained one of trust and fun, is that to put it very simply: they're really very nice and no one is a jerk. Who wants to work with jerks?

The common denominator for the people here is their sense of humor, their heart in wanting to help those more junior or in need of help, and their honest desire to do the best for their agency and their clients.

When I approached them about telling their unique story, they all had just about the same comment: "Awesome." "Great idea." "This is gonna be fun." A few even laughed and said: "Man, can you imagine the crap you're gonna see as first ads?" Yes, I could, and that's the whole point of the stories; which they all knew. You laugh and you learn.

Show the kids coming up, and the not-so-much-kids-anymore still trying to come up, that you can have the most serious stinkers the first time out, or strangest experience, and it doesn't really matter.

What matters, as the book title says, is what you learn from it. And from the lessons learned, how you go on to create work that makes the agency proud, increases your clients' market share, wins you a warehouse of awards, and then someday, have your own bizarre story to tell about your first time.

I can't wait to hear them.

*Some of our people were able to include copies or photos of their ads, or even a links to their first commercials.

A Guide To Creative Title Acronyms

(This is for anyone reading who may be a civilian – not in the ad industry). And for those of you who are in but nosey.

Some people insist that advertising has as many acronyms for their creative people as the Pentagon does for their most oblique designations. And they would be correct. But the Pentagon has a better precision ratio. So to help you fathom any acronym that may creep into the stories you're about to read, here are some basic explanations, starting from the top:

CCO: Chief Creative Officer
At larger agencies, this is the top position in the advertising infirmament. The CCO is treated like a god, and is appreciative of being remembered during Christmas and/or Yom Kippur.

The CCO is held responsible for the entire creative output of the agency, is held hostage by every client, and, in basic truth, just wants to be held.

ECD: Executive Creative Director
In some agencies, the top creative position. And as the title states, is the one who executes the creative directors.

GCD: Group Creative Director
This person is responsible for a group of accounts and a group of creative teams who are responsible for the creative product for those accounts. However, these teams will only group around their GCD with of the Ides of March in mind.

CD: Creative Director
At smaller agencies, this is the top creative person, in charge of all accounts and all creatives.

At larger shops, the CD manages an account or two, a team or two, and is the first to group around the GCD on the Ides of March. Seeing a pattern here?

ACD: Associate Creative Director
The only people who will associate with the creative director.

CW: Copywriter
This is one half of a creative team; the one who flunked English, was thrown out of journalism school, and who's grasp of basic punctuation makes what they've written look like cuneiform on a bad day.

AD: Art Director
The other half of a creative team; the one who sits and draws pretty pictures all day while growing a moustache like Salvador Dali, a beard like Leonardo DaVinci, and acts like Duchamps' "Nude Descending A Staircase".

So there you have it, the basic explanations of who does what. And who does what to whom.

And now, the totally true stories...

David Angelo
Founder, Chairman and Chief Creative Officer of David&Goliath

An American Advertising Federation Hall of Achievement inductee, David has consistently developed innovative, effective and highly creative advertising solutions for a diverse list of marketers. These include Coca-Cola, Kia Motors, Bacardi, Michelin, Lexus, Reebok, Little Caesars, and the New York State Lottery. He started his career in 1989 at DDB/New York, later served as VP/ACD at Chiat\Day, New York, and eventually joined Cliff Freeman & Partners as Executive Creative Director. In 1999, he founded David&Goliath Advertising in the belief that he could create a strong agency culture capable of taking on the industry's toughest marketing challenges. Over the years, David has created a memorable body of work that has garnered more than 300 of the industry's most prestigious awards, including Cannes Gold Lions, One Show Pencils, Clios, Effies, LA's Entrepreneur of the Year, and AdAge's Small Agency of the Year. David is a current mentor and guest speaker for the AAAAs.

David Angelo, My Thoughts

This is rather a sensitive topic, because the first time I spoke with David back in '97, his mother was gravely ill and David couldn't do anything because of the situation. He had gone into some detail and I left him with my best wishes for his mother's recovery.

What struck me about the conversation was that this was the first time we had ever spoken. I was a complete stranger. But David had felt the need to reach out to share what was troubling him so. And yet here was a man who was doing some of the funniest, most inventive TV at the time, someone anyone on the outside would never suspect of such intense sensitivity. The old "you can't judge a book by its cover" adage.

When I reminded David of this recently, at first he didn't remember. Then he asked: "I told you all that?" Yes, he had. As we spoke further, David remembered the conversation but couldn't believe he had really been so open. I read the details back to him and I could practically hear him shaking his head about it.

I then told him about our next conversation and what he had wanted if he made a move. The comp, the kind of situation where he could make a difference, where he could help create something that he could be proud of, that he could believe in; and would have other people believe in. He told me about how he wanted like-minded, passionate people around him, people who shared his vision.

Funny, David got everything he wanted.

He also got the most important thing he wanted: his mother recovered and is happy and healthy and with us today.

My First Time
By David Angelo

The Unforgettable First.

It began in the fall of 1989. I had just moved to New York City, a place I had never visited, to take a job as a junior art director on Madison Avenue for one of the greatest ad agencies of all time: DDB. It was a dream that I longed for all throughout college and a chance to bring my creative thinking to life at the official home of creativity. Of course, I really had no idea what to expect from my first agency job. I knew I'd be working endless hours, "assisting" others in the creative department, but the thought of producing my own TV campaign was the furthest thing from my mind. In school, we were all conditioned to believe that the chance of a junior working on a television commercial was about as slim as the Cubs winning the World Series. So naturally, when I was given a TV assignment in my first few months, I jumped on it. My partner and I concepted 24/7 and after a few weeks, we landed on a pretty cool idea. And after a month of going through the gauntlet of the agency and the client firing squad, our idea survived and was approved to move forward.

It was an awesome feeling. My first real TV campaign. I still love the sound of that today. Immediately, I called my parents, friends, and anyone else who would listen to the good news. They were genuinely happy for me, especially knowing how hard I worked to get there and how important a TV campaign is to a junior creative. Then it was time to get to work. We went through the process of looking at director reels, listening to music samples, and writing casting and location descriptions. It all felt very "Hollywood" to me – the thought of talking to directors and actors was something I never entertained growing up. I grew up admiring it from afar – just like any kid from a blue-collar town would do. But the fact I would travel to another city, like LA, stay in a hotel for free, eat at great restaurants, and enjoy all the other perks that come with production, left a huge glow on my face throughout the entire process. It was that moment that I felt very fortunate to be doing what I'm doing; especially since it was something I love doing.

After making all the key decisions, we packed our bags and headed out west for Tinseltown. Upon landing, we were met at the airport by a production assistant who was actually holding a sign with our name printed on it. The smile on my face kept getting bigger. The following events felt like a whirlwind– casting callbacks, scouting, and wardrobe selection all before a quickly approaching client pre-pro. There wasn't a lot of time to play, but considering what I was doing, this was play.

Following a very smooth pre-pro, the time had arrived to lock down cameras and bring our baby to life. The next morning we arrived at Paramount Studios and as I walked in, I couldn't believe my eyes – the hustle and bustle of a live set in one of Hollywood's oldest studios. The day quickly went into action. Watching sets go up, actors performing, people screaming – it was a lot to take in all at once. During a moment of down time, I grabbed an apple box and sat down. It was a very peaceful feeling. One that I'll never forget. The director noticed me just sitting there and grabbed an apple box and sat down right next to me. He asked me if everything was okay and if I was happy with the way things were going. I looked at him and very calmly said "A few weeks ago, I was in the bathroom at work when I came up with a germ of an idea that we're currently shooting. And now, all of sudden these ladders are here. That cable. Those actors. The trucks outside. And all those free cokes in the cooler are all here...all because I had to go to the bathroom."

He looked at me and smiled. It was at that moment, that I realized the power of an idea and how quickly it comes to life. I promised myself I would never forget that feeling, that I would appreciate what it takes to produce something – the effort, the money, the time, and would always relish alone time in the bathroom.

After we wrapped, we flew back home and spent two weeks in the edit. Only to have my ECD, a very tough, yet highly respected creative, tell me that I dropped the ball on the campaign – in other words, it sucked! That's advertising. A few days later, he pulled me aside and gave me a tough love kick in the ass. He told me that if I didn't get my shit together, I'd be on the next flight back to San Fran. A few months later, I got a brief to work on the New York State Lottery. We sold the campaign, produced it and won many awards.

This is my story of my first commercial – and after a few hundred later, I tell all my juniors two things:

1. Don't forget that feeling. Take in every aspect of the production. Take in the journey that brings it all to life. Remember, you worked really hard and jumped through some major obstacles to get to that set. Make it count. Who knows, maybe one day you'll write about it.

2. Don't ever show up on set with a hangover. Get to bed early.

Rosie Arnold
Deputy Executive Creative Director of BBH, London, President, D&AD

Rosie started moonlighting at a tiny creative hot shop called Bartle Bogle Hegarty in 1983 while studying at Central St Martins. She has been there ever since. Always motivated by the opportunity to do mould breaking creative work amongst like-minded people, she has had no reason to move.

She spent the formative years of her career working closely with John Hegarty, learning the trade. In her time to date she has been responsible for some of the Agency's most iconic work from Pretty Polly and Levi's in the 80s; The Independent, TAG, Robinsons and Omo. She lead Axe (Lynx) for 14 years and more recently is behind the latest phenomenon that is Yeo Valley.

Her work has amassed many awards including six Cannes Gold, six D&AD pencils and three Campaign Golds.

Rosie Arnold, My Thoughts

Now this may sound hyperbolic, but if Rosie were weather, she'd be the lightly falling gentle dew, sprinkling creative life wherever she landed.

That's not purple poetry, that's just Rosie. Her name reflects her disposition, her outlook on life, and how people feel who have the good fortune to know her, work with her, interact with her.

She's a creative magician. Not just in the manner of her ideas, but in her manner with teams who may struggle for their own. There's a photo of Rosie I saw, with her flicking away a golden cloth from an empty birdcage; which to me epitomizes her magic: she frees ideas to take flight. Houdini, move over.

She also has enough energy to power the entire UK for the next decade.

And while we've only met once, when we speak or email each other, I get the feeling that we've been friends forever; such is her honest manner.

When she began writing her story, Rosie, coming from an art background, was concerned that she couldn't write a story in a compelling manner.

But what she doesn't realize is that her Rosie story is being written every day. And that there's nothing more compelling than that.

My First Time
By Rosie Arnold

Having managed to land myself a job in a tiny creative hot shop called Bartle Bogle Hegarty, the next thing I had to do was come up with a fantastic campaign that would make John Hegarty proud of me and send my career into giddying heights and win me a much coveted D&AD yellow pencil.

Clasping my 6 layouts for a Pretty Polly stocking print campaign - dreams of walking up to podiums in my mind - I entered the meeting room to present my treasured idea.

The client who I have conveniently forgotten, systematically destroyed those dreams. He found it difficult to imagine why Venice was remotely glamorous as a location, why weren't we showing acres of leg, and what were we doing aiming the campaign at women?

Lesson No. 1 - A wise head keepeth a still tongue
The client also couldn't quite understand that I was an art director and not a secretary or a bit of fluff laid on for his entertainment.

Lesson No. 2 - There are not many women in the creative side of the business and it is not a good idea to slap a client

Somehow despite the inauspicious start, we sold the work and I found myself in heaven choosing a photographer - anyone I liked!

I asked my group head Graham Watson for his recommendations, poured over magazines, went to galleries, etc. until I had quite a list. We called all the portfolios in and so I wouldn't be influenced by a famous name I removed all the names form the portfolios before going through them.

Lesson No. 3 - Don't EVER do this again –
Unless you want to spend dizzying amounts of time trying to match up the work with the name.

I chose the one I liked best and it turned out to be the statuesque and extremely famous Terence Donovan.

Lesson No. 4 - There's a reason people become famous
They really are better than other people and that's why they become famous.

My joy and disbelief that this was a real job, and that it was mine, knew no bounds.

I was going to Venice with Terence Donovan to shoot a print campaign, and the stylist was a certain Liz Tilberis, the then-editor of British Vogue. Gulp.

Lesson No. 5 - This is the best job in the world
And however junior you are you get incredible opportunities.

Arriving in Venice and talking to our model I discovered that she and I were the same age but she was being paid more for 3 days work than I was getting for 2 years.

Lesson No. 6 - Maybe it isn't the best job in the world

It was November and the streets were flooded, no not the canals, the streets. Everything was closing up and romantic though it undoubtedly was, we couldn't get a permit. Terence had an idea. He sent the model, Liz, and the make-up artist into the Ca D'Oro on the Grand Canal.

The model wore her gorgeous evening gown and patterned tights disguised under a cloak with instructions to slip through security and out on to the balcony - we would be waiting on the opposite side, camera at the ready.

Lesson No. 7 - You need to be brave determined and inventive to get the perfect shot

He dressed me up and I posed on the opposite side of the canal and amazingly the model slipped through security and appeared on the balcony, Terence, dressed in full army camouflage (quite why in the middle of Venice I will never know), swung the camera round and photographed our model. I was 22 (just) and found the whole experience dazzling.

The shot was perfect.

Triumphantly we returned home and although the campaign was only nominated for a pencil, just getting in the book was a thrill for me and my then partner, Kiki Kendrick.

However there was an unexpected side to the shoot that both Kiki and I had to deal with and (watch out girls) it seemed to happen a lot throughout my career: unwelcome attention from guys who believe that just because you're out of the country you're fair game. It wasn't really a problem, because I was very clear that was not a path I was going to follow.

I look back now and laugh at some of the more outrageous things that were said to me, like: "I could pull you on like a wet wellington."!! UGH!. But at the time it could be intimidating. I hope that these days everyone has moved on. But be prepared.

Last Lesson- You can be bubbly, enthusiastic, care about your appearance but make sure you have a good range of charming rebuttals up your sleeves.

I realise just how lucky I was to have landed my first job at a place like BBH. I'm still here and each new project still has the thrill of my first time.

Last lesson - Do things because they interest or excite you, and interesting and exciting things will happen to you.

Nick Bailey
Executive Creative Director, AKQA Amsterdam

Named by Adweek in 2011 as one of the world's top ten creative minds in digital, Nick Bailey leads the creative output of AKQA's Amsterdam office, servicing Nike, EA Sports, Heineken, Diageo and Tommy Hilfiger. Bailey's work has been recognized with over 70 international awards, including most recently Cannes Gold, D&AD yellow pencil and Creative Review Best in Book for Heineken Star Player, a world-first dual-screen mobile and social football game. Nick joined AKQA in 2004 as Lead writer on the Nike Account, where he created some of the brand's most awarded work including Nike Photo iD, Supersonic and Nike Live. Prior to AKQA Bailey worked at LBi on Mercedes Benz, Abbey, BT and Vodafone.

Nick Bailey, My Thoughts

Nick is one of those people I don't know very well, and yet, I know him very well.

Along with Yacco Vijn, another friend and contributor to MFT from Amsterdam, they opened their arms (so to speak) to greet the new kid on the block, Ron Smrczek, the new ECD of TAXI, there.

Ron and his family were moving out there, didn't know anyone, so I said I'd introduce him to some friends and colleagues in Amsterdam. I called Nick, Yacco, and some others and they all said, great, the more the merrier and Ron was adopted. Which is nice because now he's Ron Smrczek Bailey Vijn.

Just look at Nick's picture. Isn't that a warm and inviting kisser? You should see some of the photos he posts on Facebook. But that's Nick. He's full of life and fun and knows the digital creative world inside out. Which can be a problem if you're prone to seasickness.

Nick has so many awards under his belt it's hard to sit down. And he gives some people the wrong idea when he walks. But when you're literally one of the ten top digital creatives in the world (his bio says so and it's right), you can walk anywhere and any way you want.

My First Time
By Nick Bailey

Looking back at my first commercial assignment now feels like looking back at the crew of Columbus' first expedition landing on the beaches of Cuba, confident in the belief that they were in China. We had found the Internet and, agencies and clients alike, immediately assumed it to be a version of something already familiar. Exactly what this was, the mists of time have obscured - but what comes vaguely into focus is a cross between a more sophisticated Teletext service and an on-demand entertainment channel.

Social networking, user generated content, even 'viral marketing' were forms of words as-yet unspoken. The money-tap which, back then in 1998 was open to its fullest extent, was being supplied by the same small elite who had controlled the flow of information since the birth of television, and who assumed that here was another opportunity to distribute their message to an unsuspecting, passive public. The idea, I'm sure, that this unsuspecting, passive public would take this new technology and use it to make brands of themselves, revolutionise the music and publishing industries, and even overthrow governments would have sent them running for the hills.

It was into this context that I, as a very green, very idealistic Fine Arts graduate, blundered. I had landed a job in a five-person Internet start-up because I'd written an amusing email to them on the basis of which they decided I was a potential writer. They had asked me to pen the scripts for a South-Park derived Flash-Animated cartoon about the England football team called 'WembleyPark', which they hoped they might monetize somehow. I know it seems inconceivable now that a company would hire a graduate with no experience, on a salary, to develop an idea with no immediate prospect of commercial exploitation – all I can say is that at the time, it seemed perfectly natural and rational, because everyone was doing it; which is one of the reasons why the history of bubbles, booms and busts is destined endlessly to repeat itself, I suppose.

I should also say that at the time you could write what I knew about football on the back of a Motorola Star-Tac and still have room for the lyrics to 'Wannabe'. That didn't seem to bother my employers much, which may be why 'Wembley Park' ended up being like a slightly camp cross between "Footballers' Wives" and 'Spitting Image', with a prominent role for a screechy Victoria Beckham whom our VO artist (friend of a friend) gave a voice to, not unlike that of the Mother in 'The Life of Brian'.

Now, I've said 'Wembley Park' was my first commercial assignment and, despite its appearance of being an insane vanity project, this is precisely what it became when we sold ten episodes of the show to the then brand-new UK TV channel E4, a satellite and cable entertainment spin-off of the national terrestrial station Channel 4.

E4 had decided that theirs was going to be the first truly digital, interactive station, and had embarked on a large-scale online 'content hub' at E4.com. The plan was to build and run the platform just like a TV channel: they would buy content (flash animated cartoons, as most of the country was still on a dial-up so online video was still only for very patient consumers of porn), 'broadcast' it at regular times and then make it available for on-demand viewing – or as 'on-demand' as a dial-up can be; with usually a good five minutes of buffering for the 3 or 4MB our five minutes of vector animations and uber-compressed audio demanded. The hub itself was extraordinarily technically ambitious, with floating, draggable DHTML menus and so forth. Everyone was terribly excited about it. No one asked what the revenue model was.

Our weekly shows were supposed to be topical, so we embarked on a frenetic 3-month production schedule of writing, cursory client reviews, which usually amounted to a nod with no amends (no-one seemed to care much about quality or rigour, we were all just having too much fun), and production. We had a bemused former 'Dangermouse' animator (the oldest person I knew other than family at a venerable 45) doing the characters, me on the backgrounds and sound-mix and our Man-of-Many-Voices recording each episode on, as far as I recall, a domestic mic and minidisc recorder, in one of our very un-soundproofed meeting rooms.

While we were busy creating what we, in our innocence, believed to be comedy gold, the content hub project itself was duly hitting the buffers of unanticipated technical complexities, delays and complications, which are inevitable in any large complex build but which were, to a 1990s TV executive, an unwelcome new reality.

I don't want to malign the agency who were building it, the name of which I don't recall, because I'm sure they were doing an excellent job; however all I remember is sitting in meeting after meeting at what seemed to me then the very glamorous boardrooms of E4, while the explanations of earnest technical PMs were met with baffled incredulity by the clients. 'None of us really understands what we're doing, or why', I remember thinking to myself – and I'm certain that everyone around the table was having the same thought.

Of course, in the end, we all turned out to be right. We'd allowed a kind of optimistic groupthink to lead us to sacrifice countless hours and mountains of treasure in the creation of something that no one really wanted. No one had thought to ask, 'why?' It was a great lesson to learn right at the start of my career: that if something feels not quite right, it isn't right; that if there is no rational answer to the questions, 'why?'; 'why would anyone want this?'; 'Why does this add value?' we should not proceed.

It turned out to be immediately useful when, a few short months later, the E4 hub and countless projects like it were saved from themselves by the dotcom crash, and we, (thankfully with jobs protected by our financial services clients), had to turn our hands to making work that actually paid.

I lost all the episodes of Wembley Park long ago on a corrupted drive. I have to say I'm glad; I'm sure they wouldn't have stood the test of time and I prefer my rather idealized memory of the day when, as part of a 'best of the web' round up on E4 television, an episode was broadcast to the nation. And I (and possibly a few thousand other people) saw our absurd Victoria Beckham caricature screeching out of our big old CRT TVs; the medium to which she naturally belonged.

Roger Baldacci
EVP, Executive Creative Director, Arnold Worldwide

Roger has worked at the Boston headquarters of Arnold Worldwide for twelve years and currently runs Carnival Cruise Lines among his other duties as ECD.

Prior to joining Arnold, Roger worked at Fallon in Minneapolis. Throughout his career, he has been fortunate to help build iconic brands including BMW, Volkswagen, ESPN, Miller Lite, Converse, Timberland, Nikon and truth, the nation's most successful teen tobacco control campaign.

Roger has written some of truth's more iconic commercials like "Singing Cowboy" and the "Shards O' Glass" Super Bowl spot that won him an Emmy. With three commercials on permanent display at New York's Museum of Modern Art, Gold Cannes Lions, 15 One Show pencils, and a slew of Clios, London International, NY Art Directors, Communication Arts, Radio Mercury, Kellys, and yes the Grande Effie, Roger is among the most awarded creatives at Arnold. His One Show Awards box set (I am "In" this book) became a best seller and his "Apple 1984 Focus Group" short film lampooning focus groups became an instant hit within the industry.

Roger has judged The One Show, London International, NY Art Directors, AICP and Communication Arts and speaks on advertising at Boston area universities. He lives in the suburbs of Boston with his wife Lynn, daughters Julia and Olivia and Isabelle, their mischievous mini Australian Labradoodle.

Roger Baldacci, My Thoughts

Roger is a friend I've known for more than a decade, and only met a few months ago. Such is life.

Talk about odd couples. He's a die-hard Red Sox fan (poor thing) and I'm an ultimate Yankees fan. We hate each other. We send misshapen voodoo dolls with multiple pins stuck throughout to each other, and bury each other's stolen objects in our local graveyards under full and smirking moons while incantating dark verses. We're not normal.

But other than that, we agree totally on the best advertising. He creating it, and me appreciating what he creates; as does everyone. Which is easy, because Roger has done such incredible work over the years.

He was one of the original people on one of the most impactful social campaigns in history: the original Truth campaign. And he ran that campaign for many years. That alone would be enough to have him rest on his laurels. But Roger isn't the resting type.

As affable and approachable as he is, he won't accept anything less than the best ideas possible. He'll push and prod and poke his people, but proves that you can still be a really nice guy and run major pieces of business without giving anyone else the business.

He's also a Bostonian. Which brings me back to the Red Sox thing. But even someone like Roger has to have something askew.

My First Time
By Roger Baldacci

When Phil asked me to write a story about my first time in advertising, I drew a blank. That was a long time ago. Advertising can both keep you young and age you at the same time. My memory isn't what it used to be back when I had two percent body fat. So instead of eating lunch at my desk during a conference call while simultaneously responding to emails and approving work, I walked outside and really thought about it.

And the story I finally recalled isn't so much a story filled with humorous anecdotes and/or embarrassing faux pas. But just a story about fearlessness, hunger and persistence. All things you still need today to propel your career in advertising.

I was a young writer looking to put a dent in the world and the award show books. My first real job was at Mullen where I got the stuff that fell through the cracks of the Timberland account—namely ad slicks. So despite being happy at Mullen, I left to join a start-up called Houston Herstek Favat, to work on the Converse account.

I'm probably 5'6" in thick-heeled boots and have never played basketball in my life. But I was hungry and fearless. And despite not knowing much more about basketball than what I watched during the Celtics championship runs in the 80s, I jumped in anyway. A friend who worked at the agency was also offered the chance to work on the account, but he declined because he wasn't into sports. And he is much taller than me. Some of the work I've done on Converse is still among my favorite to this day.

So my first big lesson in advertising was to be fearless and go out of your comfort zone. This I would need when I finally got my first TV assignment.

Before Arnold would go on to win the "Truth" account, partnered with Crispin, Porter, Bogusky, we handled the youth tobacco control account for the Massachusetts Department of Public Health (DPH.) Our positioning for DPH was the same as it would eventually be for "Truth"—an account that I would go on to run years later after a brief stint at Fallon in Minneapolis. The best way to stop teens from smoking is to prevent them from starting.

Back to my still-developing, soon-to-be-expanding comfort zone. Here's the brief: use teen girls to let teen boys know that smoking will make you less attractive to them. And there is no time and no money. So if it weren't enough that I was a short, white, suburban male writing ads primarily geared to the urban, African-American market, now I had to write like a teenage girl.

A teenage girl trying to get a boy. Awesome.

My partner and I knew that the first thing we had to cast was a hot teen girl. We were in our early 20's then, so it didn't sound as creepy as it sounds now. But that was the easy part. What would the message be?

We eventually landed on an idea that featured a girl giving you five"inside" tips on how to be more successful with girls. It was like handing over the playbook from the other team. We got the tips from talking to girls in the office and at home and just intuitively pulling from issues we've gleaned from movies and pop culture. Remember, this was before we could just Google the list on the internet.

The spot featured a young model sitting on a chair in a warehouse in Boston. Inter-cut with the live action, we used cheesy stock footage and animation which was supposed to illustrate the tips in an ironic fashion. But they were just cheap and cheesy. Our model says:

"Ok, here's five things all guys should know:
1. Don't change into something when you're around your friends. (donkey bray)
2. Ring the doorbell, don't beep the horn. (animation of finger pressing doorbell)
3. Hold the onions! (dog's mouth)
4. There's an invention called the telephone. Use it. (old rotary phone – Google it)
5. Nix the smoking. That yellow teeth, cigarette stench thing? It's not working.
You guys getting this?"

This was followed by the art card: SMOKING. WHAT'S TO LIKE?

I believe it was well-received, but it was an entirely forgettable spot. Cringe-worthy to look back on it now—like looking at a picture of you wearing a teal jacket with shoulder pads in the 80s.

But my first TV spot taught me to push myself. To work under pressure. To work with small budgets. To humbly accept all assignments. All things that are even more relevant today than they were back in the day.

Which is a good thing. Because a Vagisil brief just came across my desk.

David Baldwin
Lead Guitar, Baldwin&, Raleigh, NC

One of the most awarded copywriters and creative directors in the advertising business today, David Baldwin is the founder of the newly formed Baldwin&, a digital/advertising/content/branding thingy in Raleigh, NC. The former chairman of the One Club in NYC, David was also an executive producer for the Emmy-winning documentary Art & Copy, and an associate producer on the documentary The Loving Story. Among many other awards, David has been honored with 'Agency of the Year,' 'Integrated Campaign of the Year,' 'Top 25 Campaigns of the Decade' and most recently 'Small Agency Campaign of the Year.' His work and writings have been featured in many industry publications and two college textbooks.

David Baldwin, My Thoughts

I began badgering Baldwin about opportunities back in 1998.

At the time, he was already ECD of McKinney & Silver, one of the more highly respected agencies in the South and in the country, as well. Especially noted for its incredible print campaigns.

David would listen very carefully, weighing the pros and cons of the various and sundry positions I layed out before him like a Tadjiki rug salesman unfurling his wares on a golden carpet before a dazed and awestruck buyer.

But since David wasn't awestruck or dazed, and I'm not Tadjiki, it didn't work.

What did work was a relationship built on humor, trust, and the common love of our business. And that David, being the ultra-good guy that he is, would always try to help by referring certain colleagues to me for the positions I was calling him about. And though some, as it turned out, had just been convicted of major felonies and would be out of the ad business for a while, others were not unpromising. I could just imagine that evil light in his eye as he imagined me calling one of these referrals and getting Judge Judy on the line. Way to go, David.

When David was morphing from M&S to Lead Guitar at Baldwin &, he would fill me in on projects and possibilities, and I would happily applaud and cheer him on from New York.

But sometimes, that's just what friends need. And a good lawyer.

My First Time
By David Baldwin

The joke goes:
> "Know how you can tell if someone is from Texas?"
> "Because they'll fucking tell you."

That was me. I left Texas to move to New York City in June of 1985, just a few weeks after I graduated from The University of Texas advertising program, now called Texas Creative. Full of piss and vinegar, and probably salsa, I couldn't wait to get to the city and show them what I was made of. I had already been flown up for an interview at Dancer, Fitzgerald, Sample through Maxine Paetro's creative program and though I didn't get the job I was confident it was only a matter of time.

I had already been offered a job at the Richards group in Dallas, TX, by Stan Richards himself but I knew that NY was where I wanted to take this thing and come hell or high water I was going to make it there. I was so green I didn't realize what an honor it was to even be able to meet and talk to Stan, much less to be taken seriously by him. But I figured I had enough money to make it about two months in NY, I'd crash on people's floors, find a job and get my career going.

What they didn't tell me in ad school was that everyone leaves town during the summer in New York. After all, it's something like 120 degrees down on the subway platforms, (the cars weren't air conditioned at the time either) and it seemed anyone with the authority to hire me was either on the Jersey Shore, The Hamptons or somewhere in France.

So there I was, wandering the streets and avenues carrying these little briefcases with my portfolio in them and sweating all the way through a really bad suit. You didn't carry your book on a flash drive or send someone a url back then. There was no internet, no email, no way to contact people other than to call or write. You sent your book by mail or you carried it over to an agency, dropped it off and then, depending how many copies you had, you waited for it to free up. Then on to the next place.

It was a very strange game of roulette. By the time you heard about a job opening somewhere it was already too late because first you had to hunt down your book wherever it sat languishing only to find out the person who had it wasn't there, "They're in the Hamptons for the week and will be back next Monday. Please hold."

And as far as my book went, let's just say it wasn't stellar. An arsenal of puns and corny jokes, I think my best ad was for Contact cold medicine and featured a pill with little bomb fins and the headline, "The ultimate weapon in the cold war." And that was the good one.

I had decent interviews, bad interviews, embarrassing interviews. One creative director got a phone call from a friend while I was showing him my book and he took the call. The one side of the conversation I could hear went something like this.

"Hey, man. Yep, no I'm busy. .....I'm looking at a kid's book....Ha, ha, um, he's very...nice...Ha ha, yes. Okay, gotta go."

Ooph, I was very nice. Kind of like being told by your prom date that she just wants to be friends.

Another notable interview was with a guy named Joe Smith. He worked with George Lois who was one of my heroes. It was a nightmare, the guy actually made me read my headlines to him out loud and then would interrupt me in the middle and yell, "No! Too long! Think about 'Jaws.' it said the entire movie in one word. Your headlines are too long!" He went on to tell me that I didn't have what it takes and that I should reconsider my career.

Then as now, you'll meet the nicest people and you'll come across the biggest douche-bags. I guess I went to Metropolis thinking I was Superman, but my portfolio turned out to be kryptonite.

Cut to two months later, I didn't have enough money to stay, I didn't have enough money to leave. I started looking for jobs at art stores and even contemplated waiting tables, which I had no experience doing. I was staying in a one bedroom apartment with three other friends from Texas, two of whom had already gotten jobs out of school and nerves were frayed because it's hard to pack four adults into a one bedroom apartment when two of us weren't paying for anything other than food. The guys were saints but you can only be pushed so far.

I kept at it, interviewing at agencies and art stores. But then the clouds parted, the angels sang in the form of a ringing phone. Two agencies called on the same day. One was Lord Gellar Federico and Einstein offering me a job in the mailroom and the other was an agency called McCaffrey/McCall with a gig as a copywriter. Hell yes, I'll take that one.

McCaffrey and McCall was a medium sized agency for the time which meant a hundred or so people but I don't really remember the amount, it just seemed big to me at the time. David McCall was an early protege of David Ogilvy and had been one of Ogivly's copy chiefs. Amongst other things, the agency had produced work for Mercedes, Norelco and had even created *Schoolhouse Rock* for ABC. If you remember the black and white spot of Santa Claus riding through the snow on an electric razor, that was them. At the time I believe it was the longest running commercial on television.

Mostly incredibly nice, smart people were there that I still keep in touch with to this day. Certainly nothing like the shenanigans of my interview experiences.

Looking at it now, it's clear that the agency was one in transition from the old world of 15% media commissions (man, agencies made a lot of dough back then) to the newer model of fees and consolidation. In fact, not many years later the agency was acquired by Saatchi and rolled up into the mother ship, but I was long gone.

I suppose we were overstaffed because we often had nothing to do. My entire group would sit around for days and do crossword puzzles together and while that may sound fun to get paid to do nothing I found it very frustrating.

There would be flurries of activity where the entire department would work on a project for a week, produce a mountain of foam core and then go right back to doing nothing. I had this perception before getting into the business that you produced tons of work all the time but quickly realized that this is largely an industry of dead ideas. Tons and tons of dead ideas. Getting something produced was actually the exception; it was for me at McCaffrey anyway. It can take a while to build up that callus but you build it up eventually.

All the old Ogilvy rules were in evidence at the agency. (Never drop copy out of a photo, for instance.) When showing work to one of my creative directors I remember the response wasn't whether it was good or bad, he wanted to know why we were using humor? A creative director once sat me down and gave me adjectives that I should use to describe beer: Big, Bold, Clear, Clean, Crisp...all good beer words apparently.

Another thing that seems amazing to me now was how we would sometimes write copy to fit the layout. For instance, as a writer for Exxon Mobil's sponsorship campaign of the New York Symphony or some such organization, you'd write a very short headline and then the art director would lay it out and tell you how many characters to write per line for the body copy. So you'd write copy based on character length (and style of course) but you'd be asked, "Can you make the first line 24 characters and the next line 26 characters, the line after that 20 characters..." and so on. The weird thing is we used to do it and make it work. It was kind of like writing haiku with puns.

So I'd been at it awhile and had not much to show yet when I was given an assignment to do a holiday promotion for Häagen Dazs Cream Liqueur. Apparently they'd seen the success of Bailey's and thought they should get into the category. They needed small space ads to run in newspapers telling people to buy Haagen Dazs cream liqueur as a Valentine's Day gift.

There's really no secret to finding the intrinsic benefit between a cream based liqueur and Valentine's Day. Two choices, "Go out on a date and get loaded" or maybe play up the romance of it all. Shockingly, we went with the avenue that wouldn't get us sued.   The visual was a silhouette of Cupid holding a bottle of Häagen Dazs Cream Liqueur in place of a bow and arrow and the headline was:
          "Love Potion #10."

Get it? Love potion #10?, it's one better than love potion #9. It was certainly short enough that there wasn't time to yell out, "Jaws" at me if I read it aloud. Maybe Joe had taught me something after all.

I wish I could say that my first ad produced was really great and that it went on to win awards and make me famous but the truth is, it was just a little rectangular nothing; a microscopic cog in the gears of capitalism that came and went quite quickly. I suppose that so much of this business is exactly that. I will say this, I cared about that little ad and my partner and I worked really hard on it.

So the moral of this story is that you're going to be told no all the time in this business. You're going to be told you're not good enough and that your ideas stink. But you should never give up, never despair and realize that if a guy like me can a write a headline like "Love Potion #10" and then go on to make a living in this business, well, then anyone can.

Jamie Barrett
Executive Creative Director/Partner/Copywriter, Goodby Silverstein & Partners

Jamie began his advertising career in 1986 as a junior account person at Fallon McElligott in Minneapolis. In 1990, he left for Portland, Oregon where he began an eight-year run at Wieden & Kennedy. In 1998, Jamie joined Fallon, NY as a Partner and Executive Creative Director. Within two years the shop had won four Cannes Gold Lions, and its billings had quintupled to $250 million. In 2000, Jamie was named *Adweek's* National Creative Director of the Year.

In January 2002, Jamie and his family relocated to Goodby, Silverstein & Partners in San Francisco. In 2006, Jamie was named one of Creativity's Top 50 creatives and Goodby, Silverstein & Partners was honored as 2006 Agency of the Year by both *Adweek* and *Creativity* magazines. In 2007, Jamie was again named one of Creativity's Top 50 creatives and Goodby, Silverstein & Partners was honored Agency of the Year by Adweek, Ad Age, and Boards magazine. Comcast's "Rabbit" was the world's most awarded commercial, according to Ad Age's Creativity magazine. And the NBA's "There Can Be Only One" campaign won a Cannes Lion as well as being parodied by Saturday Night Live and on the cover of Time magazine.

Jamie was a Partner and Creative Director on Comcast, Chevrolet, Corona Light and the NBA. He is also a rapidly fading squash and tennis player who complains constantly about a bad back. At press time, Jamie announced plans to launch a new agency in the fall.

Jamie Barrett, My Thoughts

Except for Goodby and Silverstein, Jamie was the most senior creative at one of the best agencies in the world. He just left to begin his own agency and it was the biggest shock to hit San Fran since 1906.

But how did he do it? How many bodies did he step on and kick and mangle to slash his way to the top?

None. Nada. Zip. And that's the whole story.

Though Jamie and I have only spoken a few times over the years, here was one of the most senior creatives in the world asking forgiveness for his delinquency in not delivering his story in a timely manner.

How's that for being polite? Or massive Judeo-Christian guilt?

People who work, or have worked, for Jamie, all tell me the same thing: that he's a great guy to work with and for; and if Jamie asked them to jump off the Golden Gate Bridge they'd tell *him* to go jump. There is a limit, you know.

But other than jumping off bridges, Jamie has managed to keep his people, his clients, his global colleagues, and his Goodby and his Silverstein, very happy indeed.

The campaigns done under his aegis are creative classics.

John Updike once said about Ted Williams' un-fan-friendliness: "Gods don't answer letters."

Jamie does. Which makes him very un-Ted Williams. But that's OK, because though Jamie can't hit .406, Ted never created a great commercial.

So they're even.

My First Time
By Jamie Barrett

I think I'll give you a whole bunch of first times, if that's okay.

My first interview was at J. Walter Thompson in New York. It was an informational interview with the head account guy on Burger King, a friend of my Dad's. I asked him what the departments were at an ad agency and he said there were many, but that I would be in account services. He had a nice watch and sat behind a large desk, so I took his word for it.

My first rejection was also at J. Walter Thompson in New York. My Dad's friend felt I "should be an account man", but could see with equal clarity that I should not be an account man at a firm like his.

This first rejection was followed by twenty-two more at every multi-syllabic agency in New York in 1984. I should've kept all the letters. I could've made them into the first "0 for 23 Job Applications" coffee table book.

My first job was as an assistant account executive at Fallon McElligott Rice in Minneapolis. Years later, Pat Fallon was quoted in the press calling me "the worst account person in the history of the agency". I wish he had been kidding.

My first spec ad was one I wrote for Murray's, a bakery located right in Fallon's lobby. I used an attention-grabbing picture of a Rolls Royce, topped by the gut-buster headline "WE MAKE THE SECOND BEST ROLLS IN THE WORLD".

Having penned that gem, I realized I had a gift and kept going. I wrote a campaign for a local tanning salon featuring timeless classics like "OUR TANNING SALON IS A SHADE BETTER THAN THEIRS" and "OTHER TANNING SALONS PALE BY COMPARISON". And of course, who can forget "PEOPLE WHO LIVE THROUGH OUR WINTER OUGHT TO BE BRONZED".

Incredibly, those four bursts of genius helped me secure my second "first" job, as a junior writer at Fallon. My eternal thanks go to Tom McElligott, Pat Fallon, Nancy Rice, Fred Senn and Irv Fish—five otherwise discerning people who saw something in the pile 'o puns I showed them 25 years ago. I suspect they were simply looking for a department where I might do less damage.

My first creative presentation was a winner. I had never been in a room with a client, much less seen someone present an ad. After the account guy set things up, all eyes turned to me. What to do? The last time I'd shown a piece of creative work was in first grade. I'd drawn a picture with crayons. I wanted to show it to my Mom, so I handed it to her. I decided to go with this proven technique, and wordlessly handed my layout to the client.

My first real. actual, produced piece of work? It was a print ad for WFLD-TV in Chicago, and featured a close-up of Michael Jordan with his tongue hanging out, with the headline "WATCH MICHAEL JORDAN DRIBBLE". I was now on a pretty serious roll. (In hindsight, I'm surprised I didn't craft that last sentence into a headline for Murray's Bakery.)

I was also having some success. And the truth is, I'd probably still be spitting out rimshot puns to this day were it not for my first influences. People like Mike Lescarbeau and Bob Barrie at Fallon. Dan Wieden, Jerry Cronin and Jim Riswold at Wieden and Kennedy. These were people conceiving work that didn't fit my definition of advertising, which in turn made me more passionate about pursuing it.

Interestingly, my first real conflict in advertising was also with Jim. We didn't always see things the same way. But conflict and competition led me to conceptual places I otherwise would never have gone. And for that I am, first and foremost, thankful.

There've been other firsts. I met my first (and forever) wife in advertising. I had my first (and so far only) trips to Russia, Africa, the Ukraine, New Zealand, Sweden, Uruguay and Iceland in advertising. And in just a few months from this writing, I will be working at the first advertising agency that I can say I started myself.

So what lesson can I draw from all these firsts?

Maybe just that. That advertising is a place where the firsts keep coming. Where the newness and the couldn't-have-anticipated-that-edness of it all just never stops happening.

It helps, actually, to write about it.

Because I think for the first time, I'm finally starting to realize why I love advertising so darn much.

Interesting. Another first.

Wayne Best
Co-Founder, Cog NYC

Wayne is the co-founder of Cog NYC, where he's helping brands blur the line between advertising and entertainment. Prior to founding Cog NYC he was Executive Creative Director at JWT where he created the primetime CBS animated holiday special Yes, Virginia for Macys, as well as campaigns for JetBlue and Cadbury.

Wayne has worked at TAXI, Fallon, Wieden + Kennedy, Kirshenbaum + Bond, Cliff Freeman & Partners, Ammirati & Puris and, well, N.W. Ayer. His clients have included ESPN, Starbucks, Pepsi, Virgin Mobile, Coca-Cola, Time Magazine, Fox Sports and many others.

His work has won Cannes Lions, One Show pencils, Effie's and many other awards. Creativity Magazine called his Virgin Mobile "Chrismahanukwazakah" commercial the best holiday spot of all time. Last year he was a jury chair for the Art Director's Club Hybrid awards, which honor the year's most innovative, game-changing work.

Wayne Best, My Thoughts

Although I've known Wayne for over ten years, it took me that long to finally find him a home and a partnership. And because it came so many years after I first introduced the two parties, the only thing I could get out of it was the satisfaction of bringing two friends together.

Big deal.

The bums haven't even taken me out for a champagne dinner. Or lunch. Or breakfast. Or snack. Nothing. Nada. Zilch.

So what did it matter that in the intervening ten years Wayne won every award conceivable or in-?

So what did it matter that my original note on his file was that his reel was the funniest I had ever seen? (I have no sense of humor)

So what did it matter that he held top positions at some of the top agencies in the world?

So what did it matter that I once gave the poor guy a choice so tough to make between a position I had offered and another he had from someone else that he heaved all over his shoes? (Jackson Pollock would've been proud)

So what does it matter that Wayne is one of the nicest people you could ever want to work with or for?

Oh, all right. It matters.
But I'm still waiting for my champagne.
I'll settle for seltzer.

My First Time
By Wayne Best

As with many "first times", the moment itself isn't all that memorable. What is memorable is the crazy adventure that leads up to that first time. The hunt. In my case, it involved working for a tyrannical publisher with Alzheimer's, filling my lungs with spray mount, driving across the country in a tiny Honda stuffed with my life's belongings, moving in with a lesbian who's dog farted constantly, and taking a job I didn't want, only to find out I was being laid-off, at the urinal.

Let's start at the beginning.

I graduated from Art Center in the middle of a recession. Although I was sure my destiny was to work for a great ad agency, I gave in and took a job at Pool & Spa News Magazine. The owner of the publication was demanding. The problem was, he also had no memory. So one day he would tell you do something and the next day he'd yell at you for doing it. He had no recollection that you were following his orders. In fact he insisted that he would never have given you that direction. I knew I had to get out.

I decided to photograph every ad I did in school and make color prints at the local Fotomat. Each week, after work, I would spray mount my ads to postcard paper and send them to 50 people in the business I admired. (Dan Wieden, Pat Fallon, Gary Goldsmith, Jeff Goodby, etc.) A few weeks into the project the Super 77 spray mount was beginning to build up in my lungs and I would find myself gasping for air in the middle of the night.

One day when I came home from my lousy job there was a message on my answering machine from Gary Goldsmith. Holy shit! The postcards worked. He wanted to see my portfolio. He also told me to connect with some recruiters. This was it, I was on the way to losing my advertising virginity.

At the time, I was dating an illustrator from Art Center and we decided it was a good idea to go to New York and start interviewing, so we booked a flight. We didn't book a room though. We were broke, so we planned to just find a youth hostile after we landed. We found one in Times Square. This was the early 90's, when it was still full of prostitutes and three-card Monty hustlers. Not exactly the place to prepare for job interviews. I still remember that every evening, around midnight, a large transvestite would start belting show tunes out the window, while others shouted for him to "shut the fuck up". This went on for hours.

It was June and New York was a humid 97 degrees. Every day I wore this horribly ill-fitting pea green Miami Vice blazer I got for graduation. Covered in flop sweat, I'd go from pay phone to pay phone setting up meetings and running all over town. I loved it.

So I finally got the job that let me do my first commercial, right? Nope.

I had some good interviews, but no offers. Within a day back at Pool & Spa Magazine I said "screw it" and quit. I decided to go NY and take my chances. I sold all of my furniture at a yard sell. And I sold my car. Then my girlfriend and I jumped in her car and drove across the country. We had the phone number of someone named Brenda, which we got from her ex-girlfriend, who came to our yard sale. She said Brenda would let us sleep on her living room floor if we helped with her rent. Even with her dog running around farting all night long it was better than the youth hostel.

So now I get my first real advertising job and shoot my first commercial, right? Not yet.

I was working at Mac Temps when I got the call from Cliff Freeman. Could I freelance? Cliff was a legend, hell yeah I could freelance. On my first day I waited at reception for 30 minutes before I realized they didn't have a receptionist. Then I wandered past the cookie jar collection and heard laughter coming from a small office. I went in and a group of the best creatives in advertising were huddled together, working on a print ad. They threw me the brief and told me to start tossing out ideas. Although it was intimidating, it was exactly what I hoped the business was like. Unfortunately, the freelance gig only lasted a couple weeks.

I had schlepped back to Mac temps to make ends meet when I got another call. A young writer at NW Ayer needed a partner. It was a terrible agency, but I would get real advertising experience and might even get to do TV.

What did I have to lose? I took the job.

They say you learn more from failure than from success. So I learned a lot at NW Ayer. It was a sad place that was rapidly falling apart. The office was full of empty desks with boxes on them. Shortly after I joined, their biggest client, AT&T, put the business into review. It was an account they'd had for over 100 years. The lower level employees were allowed to watch the pitch on close circuit TV's in a neighboring conference room. It was a disaster. At the end of the meeting the agency CEO grabbed the AT&T CEO, dragged him to a corner of the room and groveled for the business, pleading with him not to fire the agency. Of course he chose to do this right in front of a camera, so it came through huge and loud in the adjoining conference room. I'd never seen an entire room collectively wince. They lost the pitch.

A couple weeks later, while peeing at the urinal, my writer and I got the news from a senior co-worker.

        "Hey guys, sorry about that?"
        "Sorry about what?"
        "You getting laid off."
        "We're getting laid off?"
        "Oh, shit. He told me he spoke to you guys. Don't tell him I told you."

Only 6 months into the job and I was back on the street. Not only did I not sell a commercial, I didn't even have a job.

Then I received a call from Ammirati & Puris, one of the best agencies in the country at the time.

They needed a young art director to work with a kid named Ian Reichenthal who was being promoted from storyboard assistant to junior copywriter. I was booked to freelance with him for two weeks. I ended up getting the job and together we started to gain momentum and get bigger and better assignments. Eventually that lead to, you guessed it, my first TV spot.

It wasn't the world's sexiest spot. It was for some sausage breakfast sandwich at Burger King. The director was Steve Horn, who was a big deal at the time. Although the whole thing is a bit of a blur, I do remember a few things. I couldn't believe it took that many people to make a TV commercial. I couldn't believe they took my bad storyboard drawings and built a huge set based on them. And I couldn't believe that the director was constantly bickering with his wife, his executive producer, openly and loudly throughout the entire shoot.

In the end, my mom was proud and I had finally gotten a TV spot under my belt. I was no longer a TV virgin. I was officially on my way.

Now it's almost 20 years later. I've worked for Dan Wieden and Pat Fallon, I spent years working for Cliff Freeman, my son went to pre-school with Gary Goldsmith's son and we made pancakes together at the school pajama party, NW Ayer finally went out of business, my writing partner at NW Ayer became a successful actor and comedian, Times Square got rid of the prostitutes, Ian Reichenthal became an award-winning writer, and I went on to do a few hundred more commercials, including a few good ones.

Sometimes, when I take a deep breath, I think I can still feel the spray mount rattling around in my lungs, reminding me of where I started.

Robert Clifton, Jr.
Former Exective Creative Director, Burrell Communications

Robert Clifton Jr, has worked on titans like Nintendo, Kellogg's, Disney and Coke, as well as challengers like Reebok, Hefty, Land O' Lakes, Fruitopia and Famous Footwear. And while his efforts have been recognized with creative awards like Addy, Mobius, Hugo, CA, AD&D, The One Show and even made the prestigious Shots Magazine.

He is most proud of the fact that most of the very same work, withstood the torture of Milward-Brown, Ameritest and ASI. Currently, Robert spends his days and nights plying his craft on McDonald's and Toyota, in search of the elusive Cannes Lion.

Robert Clifton, Jr., My Thoughts

Robert is one of the funniest people on this, or any other, planet. On my last trip to Chicago, I stopped up to his office to say hello and for the next hour or so, Robert had me on the floor. No, literally, he had no chairs.

But other than that, he had me laughing the whole time. We began with a serious conversation of the state of advertising in Chicago and the country as a whole, and somehow, very shortly, it devolved into Robert and his sons doing this, or his sons doing that, or Robert doing that and his sons doing this. Or his wife not letting them do this *or* that.

Then he got onto his peregrine falcon tales about when he was Co-ECD of CME/Minneapolis and he would fly back and forth every weekend to be with his wife and sons. I don't know how the airlines flew in a straight line with him aboard.

My side was hurting so hard from laughing that he called in an EMS medic who quickly joined me in laughing on the floor.

I told Robert he should forget about advertising and get onto the stage of one of the great comedy clubs or groups in Chicago and let it rip. But nah, he loves advertising and his time being the ECD of the one of the most prominent agencies in the country whose specialty is advertising to the African-American and Latino markets.

You see, Robert is one of the few African-American ECDs in the country. And, unfortunately, that's no laughing matter.

My First Time
By Robert Clifton

Who in the hell is Wario?

It was 1992 and I was an associate copywriter at Leo Burnett (breaking my neck on the assignments nobody else wanted). My boss pulled me and my art director Garry Valone aside and said, "Look, it's not that I don't appreciate the fact that you had 25 concepts for the Christmas card and 30 re-designs for the Kool-Aid packages, I just don't appreciate having to look through all of it."

Which brings us to my first commercial.

I'm not sure if it was a reward for putting our all into assignments from hell or a just distraction to keep us from putting our boss through hell. Either way, it was presented to us as: two teams are out on production and another team is on vacation, leaving an empty slot for a team to work on an upcoming Super Mario Land commercial. Finally, we were getting a chance to cut our teeth on a TV assignment.

Garry and I went to work immediately. We dug up every bit of information we could find. We spread it all out on the floor of our cube and we studied it, leaving no stone unturned. It was like we were on CSI. We looked at every Nintendo commercial that had ever been done. We played the game day in and day out. And we got to know Mario-personally. Because after all, the brief said that Mario was to be the hero of this commercial. But there he was, on page 13 of the instruction booklet, a character who was in essence, the nemesis of Mario. His name-Wario. Who knew?

We went to work quickly. We had found some tension. A conflict. The stuff all great stories are made of. So we decided to have Wario, try to turn kids against their hero Mario. We chose hypnosis as his weapon, complete with a spiraling pinwheel. We even gave Wario an evil laugh-"Huhuhuhahahahaha"-which I practiced for days.

Our next hurdle: several rounds of presentations. I will never forget the words that kept coming out of everybody's mouth. When we presented to our creative director: "Who in the hell is Wario?" Our first creative review meeting with the account team: "Who in the hell is Wario?" Even when we got to the client: "Who in the hell is Wario?"

Our answer: "He's the bad guy on level 9. We haven't played that far; always run out of lives by level 4. But it's right here on page 13 of the manual."

So there our spot was, sticking out like a sore thumb. And the CEO of Nintendo loved it. Especially my evil laugh "Huhuhuhahahahaha". I'll never forget watching the discussion flow back and forth across the boardroom table, never really knowing what the outcome was, until my boss shook my hand and said, "Congratulations, son, you just sold your first spot." From there on, it only got sweeter.

Since Wario was just a bad guy with a bit part in a GameBoy game, we were charged with breathing life into him. The screen was black & white, so the first thing we had to do was add color to his overalls, to his eyes, to his mustache, even to his slobber. We wrote a character study that included in-depth info like what kind of food Wario might eat, where he might live, right down to what kind of pet he might own. Then we auditioned over 100 actors to give Wario a unique voice and deliver his trademark evil laugh: "Huhuhuhahahahaha".

Then we were off to Denver to work with Celluloid Studios (the production company that would later serve as the lab where students Matt Stone and Trey Parker would create the pilot episode of South Park). There we teamed with director James Wahlberg and took the concept from boards to pencils to cell animation.

Once we had the cell animation of Wario in the can, it was off to LA, to put the final touches on the spot. Compositing. Color correction. And my favorite - sound design with Machine Head. Leaves were crunched, eggs were cracked, oranges were thrown against walls, until we had an incredible piece of sound design. Then we all took a step back. And there it was in all its glory. My first commercial.

I'll never forget the first time I saw it on TV. I sat there, hypnotized by the wonder of it all. What started as a blank piece of paper was now a mesmerizing pinwheel, spellbinding music, and at the center of it all, Wario. It was like staring into the nursery at your first child. Kids went crazy. They all came running to defend Mario against the evil threat of Wario. The spot was dubbed into Japanese, then French, then German. But the laugh-"Huhuhuhahahahaha" - was always the same.

Before you knew it, Wario had his own game. He became a stuffed animal. A back pack. Even a pencil eraser. My baby was a star! It's was like Rocky. We just kept on creating commercial after Wario commercial. And it's all stood the test of time. I'm proud to say that if you go to youtube and search Wario, you'll find that fans from around the world have uploaded the whole collection of Wario spots, including the original-in all of it's dubbed versions.

Now nobody asks, "Who in the hell is Wario?"-Huhuhuhahahahaha.

(Here's a youtube link-check out the log line from the guy who posted it)

http://www.youtube.com/watch?v=DhB8XG9_5Rc

Jeremy Craigen
Global Executive Creative Director, VW, DDB/UK

Jeremy started his career at the now defunct Ted Bates in 1984, where he produced work of little merit. A few years later, Bates was merged in to Dorlands (now defunct) where he managed to get a couple of decent things out. In 1990 he somehow managed to get in to the hallowed offices of BMP DDB, just across the road. During those early years he worked on numerous accounts including VW, Sony and American Airlines.

In the mid 90s he was made a Creative Director on VW and helped shape the "Surprisingly Ordinary Prices" campaign into the most awarded campaign of the year and saw DDB as the most awarded agency of the year in the Gunn Reports inaugural year.

In 2003 he became Executive Creative Director of DDB/UK and has twice seen the Agency become the most awarded Agency in the world at the Gunn report. In 2012 he has decided to take on the global role of ECD on his beloved VW account.

And in March this year was awarded The Chairman's award at the British arrows for an outstanding contribution to film and television advertising. Yay!

Jeremy Craigen, My Thoughts

Jeremy needs no verbal boost from me. Since he agreed to be a contributor, he's become the Global CCO for VW (excepting N.A.), the President of DDB, and has had a baby boy, to boot.

Now I'm not taking credit for any of this (especially the baby), but what a strange coincidence.

But back to boosting Jeremy, who needs no boosting.

Jeremy actually apologized that his baby being born interfered with him writing his story. I'm not kidding. He's so nice that he actually felt he was letting MFT down. I had to give him a baby dispensation.

When I actually met Jeremy in London, in his office, he was willing to slit a vein and write in blood that he'd get his story in shortly. I gave him a "no blood oath" dispensation this time (I was beginning to feel like the Pope with so many dispensations), and began to be regaled by an expansive Jeremy telling huge-smile stories of his mileage on the VW highway, and his absolute and genuine excitement about the road ahead. I envied VW.

If Jeremy were any more relaxed and at ease with his being and his place in the advertising Olympus, he would have to be a Zen Master (which he may be, for all I know).

What I do know is that here's a man at top of his game, at top of his career, and probably on top of a huge pile of diapers, as well.

My First Time
By Jeremy Craigen

I remember, as a yet-to-be employed copywriter, looking through Campaign magazine's top twenty advertising agencies table with my, then yet-to-be employed, art director, Jeremy Carr.

We decided that there were only two agencies that we would not even consider working at from that table and duly crossed them off our lists. They were McCanns London and the now-defunct Ted Bates.

Fast forward three months and there we were, sitting at our desks at Ted Bates, somewhere off the Euston Road, a million miles from the glossy advertising world in Soho.

Now Ted Bates may have been creatively one of the worst agencies in the UK at the time (I remember a CD from a more creative agency wiping his hand on his jacket after shaking hands with me on hearing where I worked) but it was full of lovely people that all strived to do good work, but the clients there were just not interested. I've always thought since those early days that an agency is only as good as the clients it has. And in the case of Ted Bates, there wasn't one.

Jeremy and I decided to start looking for a new job after about a week. And strangely all those people who liked our book when we were students, didn't like our book when we were a junior team. Suddenly the rules had changed. So back we went to Ted Bates to improve our spec work and maybe get to make something half-decent.

I can't really remember our first ad in detail (call it selective memory!). I know it was for Matchbox pre-school toys and I know it featured babies dressed in white coats testing out the toys (yes, it was that good). I also remember it was directed by Simon Delaney who was also starting out as a director. The commercial is on neither of our reels.

I don't regret my time at Ted Bates, at all. I worked with a lot of unsung heroes, had a lot of fun, made a lot of friends and made a lot of mistakes. Mistakes that may have got me fired from one of the better agencies in town. But I also learnt a lot, too.

I learnt that people who work in less good agencies are not necessarily less good than people who work in good ones.

I learnt that producing one, half-decent ad in a bad agency (not Matchbox) will get you far more noticed than an average ad from a great one.

Most importantly, I learnt that starting off in a bad agency is not necessarily bad for your career. It could even be beneficial. It takes a certain arrogance out of you. It makes you hungrier to do great work. And more optimistic. The grass must surely be greener.....

The reality is the majority of young creatives won't start out at their agency of choice. But with a lot of hard work and a little bit of luck they might make it to the third or fourth on their list.

Susan Credle
Chief Creative Officer, Leo Burnett North America

Every agency says it wants "to do great creative," but for Chief Creative Officer Susan Credle, it's the reason why that matters.

By the time she joined Leo Burnett in the fall of 2009, she had risen at BBDO to EVP Executive Creative Director. She was known throughout the advertising industry for her reinvention and 15-year stewardship of M&M's iconic characters as well as for helping to launch Cingular Wireless and ultimately turn it into a leader brand. Along with consistently awarded work for such clients as Pepsi, FedEx, Lowe's, Bank of America and Visa.

Sharing these lessons with both veteran creatives and the top new talent she has attracted to Leo Burnett, Susan has spearheaded a creative renaissance at the agency. Her leadership, inspiration and in-the-trenches contributions have led to legacy-respecting yet forward-looking campaigns for Leo Burnett clients like McDonald's, Allstate, Kellogg's, P&G, Sealy and Invesco.

"We don't have a house style," Susan likes to say. "The work should all look unique, because each of our clients is unique."

Susan Credle, My Thoughts

Though Susan and I had spoken over the years, I could never lure her away from BBDO. She was happy and moving up against all odds in an environment where testosterone flowed like Gatorade.

She was doing incredible work, she was highly respected, and even more importantly, she was liked as much as she was respected.

When she became North American CCO for Leo Burnett, I got calls from my friends in Chicago asking what was she like; was she Scylla or Charybdis or Circe?

No, she was Susan.

In another era, she might have been dubbed a Southern Belle. And though from Dixie, she readily adapted to the D Train in New York.

When Susan and I met in her office on one of my Chicago trips, not too long after she become Leo Burnett's North American CCO, we talked about the old times in New York, but more about the new ones in Chicago. She talked about her new town and her new responsibilities. She talked about the other agencies in town and wanting to be part of that community. She was making herself at home once again.

As we sat and talked, I kept thinking it was good she was in Chicago. The warmth she generated might mitigate the weather.

When you read Susan's story, it's very open, very sensitive and extremely honest. It will not make you laugh. It will make you think.

My First Time
By Susan Fowler Credle

In 1985, I didn't know that while a one-way ticket to Newark from North Carolina was only $39, the taxi to 63rd and Park would be $50 before tip. So much for that $100 to get me started in NYC.

I didn't know that a BA in Journalism from the University of North Carolina couldn't even land you a job as a secretary (somewhere between then and now the name changed to assistant) if you were unable to type 60 wpm flawlessly. A BA in typing or bartending would have been a great asset that summer.

I didn't know that the Agency of the Year that year, which I had set my sights on, was also known as the Boys Club of Madison Avenue. And I was not a boy named Sue.

I didn't know that an $11,500 starting salary would turn out to be $350 every two weeks, which meant on top of one low-paying job, I needed a few more to make rent.

I didn't know that when I saw Mr. Dusenberry in the elevator and told him he was, indeed, Mr. Dusenberry, and he said, "Please, call me Phil" that I actually would for many, many years.

I didn't know that the boss who promised to help me become a copywriter would be replaced with a boss who didn't believe in promoting secretaries.

I didn't know that out of that frustration I would gain the courage to ask Charlie Miesmer if he would look at my marker-drawn ads (there was no such thing as a Mac) which included a very average campaign for Jelly Bellies – "carry a six-pack in the palm of your hand."

I didn't know much about baseball when I went on my first shoot. At Fenway. With Ted Williams.

I didn't know that Charlie Miesmer, who called me "Kid" for 20 years would hand me the keys to his corner office overlooking Radio City Music Hall when he retired. After all, I still did work at the Boy's Club of Madison Avenue (even though in the late 80s we moved to Sixth Avenue).

I didn't know that the younger people I came in contact with early in my career would go on to be incredible successes in this business. Most impressive Mssrs. Wall and Graff.

I didn't know people who intimidated me through out my career would become friends and not just on Facebook.

I didn't know that when I married Joe Credle in 1990, we wouldn't be able to have children.

I didn't know that as a Creative Director, I would channel all those maternal feelings into creating work with other people.

I didn't know working with walking, talking candy for 14 years would be the opposite of a career-killer and that meeting Paul Michaels in 1995 would change my life.

I didn't know when I first used the phrase "What the fuck!" how powerful it could be. But being 5'3, southern and female, I learned pretty quickly.

I didn't know how hard you had to work to be given a nickname by Lubars – Spinney thanks you, D-Tron.

I didn't know when we gave birth to a brand called Cingular in 2000, that we would marry it and bury it in nine years. Nor did I know how emotional that would be.

I didn't know a show called Mad Men would air and a lot of people would think Peggy's character was based on me even though I was learning how to ride a tricycle in the '60s.

I didn't know that in 2012 "Where are the women in advertising?" would still be a headline.

I didn't know that a career in advertising came with the opportunity, and more importantly the responsibility, to do some good in the world.

I didn't know after 24 years at BBDO NY, I would take a plane one way to Chicago to work for Tutssel at Leo Burnett.

And I didn't know that almost every day in this business would make me feel like the first time I walked into an agency. Nervous. Awed. Inspired. Excited. And damn lucky.

So what do I know after 27 years in advertising? Sometimes when you don't know what you are up against, it's harder for it to get in your way.

Jonathan Cude
Chief Creative Officer, Partner, McKinney

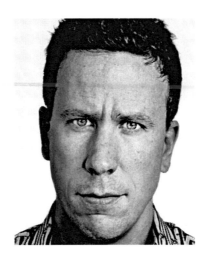

Jonathan joined McKinney in 2003 as group creative director, coming from Wieden+Kennedy, where he wrote for Nike and Diet Coke. At Wieden, he demonstrated a broad creative range, from the humor of Nike "Streaker," Creativity's runner-up for ad of the year, to the inspiring drama of the Cannes Gold Lion winner, Nike "Before." As GCD, Jonathan's teams won virtually every major award from Cannes Lions and One Show Pencils to IAB MIXX Awards (including the inaugural best of show) and four Effies for campaigns including the Audi A3 *Art of the Heist* and the Sony Bravia *The World's First Television for Men and Women.* Jonathan was named chief creative officer in 2008. He is a graduate of the University of Texas at Austin.

Jonathan Cude, My Thoughts

When David Baldwin left McKinney & Silver, Jonathan stepped up to the imperial purple of Executive Creative Director.

He had already proven his creative chops at Wieden & Kennedy and Tucker, Wayne, Lucky and had been at M&S for quite a while.

As always, our relationship began by me calling and threatening severe bodily harm if he didn't go after a senior opportunity I was working on.

And after a couple of light-hearted follow up calls on both our parts, and a restraining order from his part to my part, we settled down to a relationship of symbiotic simplicity. We never spoke to each other again.

OK, so that's not true. What is true is that the people who work for Jonathan really love working for him. Since I don't recruit into the agency, it's kosher for me to recruit out; but most of the time, the people want to stay put. It's not only the lifestyle in the Durham, N.C. area, but the culture that Jonathan has tenderly engendered. One of mutual respect, and continuous hard-working and award-winning creativity.

And in an industry where humor is coin of the realm, Jonathan must have a treasure chest buried somewhere.

My First Time
By Jonathan Cude

My first job in advertising was answering phones. I was an assistant to the Director of Broadcast Production. This was before people started using email very much – it's hard to believe that time existed, but it did. So people called. My boss didn't like voicemail. I probably took 30 phone messages a day for him.

After a while he tried to promote me to production assistant or associate producer. From what I could tell of broadcast production, at what was then called Tucker Wayne/Luckie & Co., I didn't think I wanted to do it.

So my boss, John Adams, to whom I will forever be indebted, suggested I try copywriting. Seemed like a weird idea to me. I did not consider myself a writer. I hadn't enjoyed writing papers in high school or college. And without an academic background in advertising I didn't really know what copywriters did.

Anyway, I started working on little things around the office through the kindness of some of the creatives. This eventually led me to a portfolio school in Atlanta – The Creative Circus. But before I went to school, I got a chance to do my first TV production.

I was asked if I wanted to work with a freelance creative director from New York, a guy named Ron Burkhardt. Not sure what he saw in me, except maybe someone he could get to do anything at any hour, any day. It was probably borderline abuse, but so be it.

The client was the BellSouth Yellow Pages. We came up with an idea that used Dixie Carter (who, at the time, was a big TV star on a show called "Designing Women" which happened to be set in Atlanta). The idea was that she would build a lake house and use the Yellow Pages to hire all the workers she would need to build the house.

I have literally no recollection of why we decided to use Dixie Carter. In retrospect I think it probably had something to do with why Ron was brought in to freelance at the agency in the first place. Bring in a bit of that old BBDO/New York sensibility. Find an idea, then, find the right celebrity to bring it to life (or vice versa). It seemed to make sense at the time and what did I know? I just wanted to make something, anything, happen.

What Mr. Burkhardt failed to tell me was that he had a partner back in New York. We get on the phone with him one night about 11 o'clock. I didn't know who he was. I had a vague understanding that people had "partners" but I certainly didn't have a good idea of what their roles were supposed to be.

We start talking about the idea and his partner on the other end of the phone says, "Who the fuck is that? What did you say? Who the fuck are you? Ron, who the fuck is this guy?"

It was calmly explained that I was just helping out "down here in Atlanta," no big deal. I think Ron winked at me. His partner exploded.

"That's fucking bullshit! This is amateur hour!" Which, truth be told, it was. It was a bit of an eye opener to know that people like this actually existed in the world of advertising. I'd seen people like this in movies about advertising maybe, but to be screamed at by one, live, over the phone all the way from New York City — it felt strangely like an honor. We sold the campaign to BellSouth.

At the time it didn't occur to me that people could have entire careers without working on big budget TV commercials with celebrities. Or at least it could sometimes take years to reach this point. I didn't know what I didn't know. As part of the deal Dixie, and her husband Hal Holbrooke, negotiated that BellSouth actually build them a real house on a lake in Tennessee.

The campaign was shot around the construction of the house. I was allowed to attend one day of the shoot. I drove myself up to Tennessee from Atlanta early one morning. And there she was — Dixie Carter. Saying some words that I wrote. I'm not ashamed to admit — it hooked me.

I realized advertising was what I wanted to do. It was very motivating. As someone who'd spent the six years after college, working as a stock boy, a shoe salesman and a secretary it was all pretty heady stuff.

I was offered a job at the agency as a copywriter. I turned it down.

I was naïve and dumb enough to think if I went to portfolio school I might be able to get an even better job, at a better agency.

Sometimes it pays to follow your instincts. 18 months later I was at Wieden and Kennedy.

Greg DiNoto
Partner, Chief Creative Officer, Deutsch, Inc, New York

Greg started his career at boutique Greenstone & Rabasca, and later, Bozell Inc. where he created award-winning work for a wide variety of clients including MassMutual Life Insurance, Chrysler and Merrill Lynch. In the early '90s, Greg joined Deutsch as a Group Creative Director and soon became the ECD, shaping the creative product that drove Deutsch's unprecedented growth and success with clients like IKEA, Tanqueray, Prudential Securities and Kohler. Along the way, Deutsch received National Agency of the Year status from *AdAge, Adweek, Creativity,* and *SHOOT* magazines.

Greg also ran his own agency, first as DiNoto Lee, with fellow ex- Deutscher Esther Lee and later as DiNoto Inc. There he created campaigns for many high-profile advertisers, including CNN, The Coca-Cola Company, MLB.com, GE and Burton Snowboards. He returned to Deutsch as Partner, Chief Creative Officer in November of 2009, with a mission to overhaul the agency's creative product, and to reshape its vision as a truly integrated agency.

Over the course of his career, Greg's work has been recognized by the Andy's, the Addy's, Adweek's Creative All-Stars, the Art Director's Club, the Clio's, Communication Arts, London International Awards, The Effies, Archive, D & AD, Cannes, and the One Show. Greg's natural passion for our business has made him a regular on the teaching circuit at Columbia University, FIT and Ad House. In his spare time, he enjoys skiing, motorcycling and big-game fishing.

Greg DiNoto, My Thoughts

I knew Greg during his first stint at Deutsch, Inc., back in 1997. That was before Donny had become "The Donny" (as in Deutsch); as opposed to "The Donald" (as in Trump). Personally, I prefer "The Donny". And, of course, I prefer "The Greg".

Now that Greg is a Partner and CCO of Deutsch, Inc./New York, it's been suggested that he change his name to Greg DiNotable. But that's not Greg.

Greg's one of the most honest, down-to-earth people you'll meet. You'll know that almost immediately when he opens his mouth. And the New York City expletives come flying out like furious yellow-jacks at a protein picnic. His verbiage is more salty than the Dead Sea.

Greg isn't one to mince words. He calls it as he sees it and he sees it right on target.

He's managed the amazing balancing act of being humble and CCO simultaneously. He's like a big, huggable teddy bear; but the claws can come out when the creative doesn't. The work must be the best.

He's so honest, that once, years ago when he was a partner in his own agency and I wanted to introduce him to a potential buyer, he said (and I paraphrase): "Are you nuts? It's a shell." But he didn't understand. It wasn't the accounts or fixtures to be bought, it was *him.* His creative ability, his passion, his core knowledge of creative and what it takes to produce a great campaign.

But as you see, it all worked out well anyway.

And as far as I'm concerned, everything about Greg DiNoto is notable.

My First Time
By Greg DiNoto

I'm gonna cheat. I'm not gonna give you my first time. Not exactly. My first time was lackluster. And try as I might, I couldn't conjure up something instructive, or especially inspiring about it. Instead, I'll talk about "first times" in terms of realizations about our business. For a young copywriter who wanted to make some noise, the world of advertising was built on these little epiphanies. Actually they were more like small, but ultimately, benevolent strokes.

#1. As a second year copywriter, presenting in my first new business pitch, I share an aside with my teammate, which is utterly misconstrued by our client as a comment on his substantial weight. He interrupts the meeting to accuse us of fat-hate. We did not win the business.

Realization: Our business is insane. So too, with its perpetrators. Utterly, beautifully, poetically insane. Be prepared for a decades-long orgy of "personality."

#2. I've just handed over my first piece of body copy to an account person who takes out a red pen – I've just handed over a baby harp seal to an Inuit with a club. I ask him to remind me what his title is. He says "Account Director" (he put it in initial caps), whereupon I remind him that mine is "copywriter." I urge him to drop the pen and step away from the copy -- and to allow me to address his concerns without the benefit of his mark-up.

Realization: Be open to any and all input, but stand up for yourself. It's rare that someone else will. And do it from day one.

#3. It's my first pro-bono campaign. Or at least it will be if my partner and I can sell our work.

But the work has not yet been done. And the meeting is two days away. It's "percolating" in our procrastinating brains. The client has graciously given our agency the mandate to do something great. So we pull our first all-nighter to get there. It's brutal, but productive. We make some good things.

Realization: Pressure, like fire, can be a friend.

#4. I'm on the set of my first TV campaign. My 30-second scripts are timing out like readings from the Torah. This is the first time they have been read aloud, (like the Torah) which is not good. I am hacking away at my scripts on-set, while the on-camera talent is doing her best to fist them into their half-minute slots. Of course, my creative director should share the blame in this, and thus the fix-it responsibility, but is preoccupied with convincing a young starlet that he can make balloon animals without using his hands.

Realization: Read your scripts out loud, stupid.

#5. My first major corporate campaign for a national brand... the campaign that I know is the right campaign, that I believe is the best idea presented, has just been killed by my creative director in deference to another safer one. The account director believes in my campaign and she wages war for it. It's back and breathing, and runs for 10 years.

Realization: There is no ally like a bad-ass account person.

#6. I'm at a big agency in a big conference room with 5 other creatives, and a clutch of smiling back-slappers. Our galactic creative director is presenting work to potential client, a certain bottled water client from Europe. The client is interrupting him. The client is making poopy faces. The client is insulting (not criticizing, but *insulting*... criticizing would be normal, and expected at this juncture) the work we did on spec. Over the weekend. The galactic creative director, my hero, shows the certain bottled water client from Europe the door.

Realization: Take pride in what you do. And never take the poopy face.

#7. I'm in Atlanta. Presenting work to Ted Turner. I'm sitting next to Ted Turner. It's my first time dancing for a bona-fide, billionaire badass, soul-wasting, fuckmeister of the universe. I begin to present the work to him... and he interrupts me to explain that this particular execution is "the worst piece of shit he's ever seen." I swallow something – air maybe. Then I explain that if he will indulge me, there are more pieces of shit where that came from, and begin to present execution number 2. Ted smiles.

Realization: Steady.

There are a million of these little realizations... these epiphanies that collectively help you get smart in our business. They might come from examples set by a wizened old mentor, or a competitor who is attempting to remove your liver with a warm spoon. Whatever their origin, remain open to the universe and it's small, benevolent synaptic intrusions...

Steve Doppelt
Former Executive Creative Director, EuroRSCG, New York

Steve Doppelt has spent more than twenty years working as a Writer/Creative Director at some great New York agencies and a few awful ones. Away from advertising, he has recorded numerous CDs under his singer/songwriting alter ego name Steven Mark. He lives in Manhattan where he spends his free time in the park, along the river and on the couch with his girl friend and his Basset Hound, Tyrone.

Steve Doppelt, My Thoughts

Steve Doppelt is a split personality. A computer keyboard and piano key-pounding dynamic duo trapped in one.

One minute he's a mild-mannered ECD/CW; the next, he's channeling Irving Berlin. Well maybe not Irving Berlin, but perhaps the evil spawn product if Janis Joplin had paired with Irving in one particularly booze and drug-induced coupling.

You read his bio, he even has an alias. What self-respecting creative has an alias? Perhaps a better question should be what self-respecting creative doesn't?

He even has albums on iTunes. And the music is really good, too. Not Lawrence Welk, but who is? Where does his multiple personality cum multi-talent end?

If you see his infamous advertising work, much of it is the work of the devil: gambling and beer. And insurance.

I've known Steve for seven years. Seven years of viewing his commercials by day then passing on invitations to trudge down to the Village in the middle of the night to listen to his music while I get contact highs and all sorts of interesting offers from the denizens under the tables.

It's been interesting. And, I know, it shall continue to be so.

My First Time
By Steve Doppelt

Bite & Smile.
I had such high hopes.

I wasn't going to conquer the advertising world. I was going to use it as a springboard to bigger things; better things like screenplays, plays, and sitcoms. After all, it had been the TV show "Bosom Buddies" that had inspired me to go into advertising in the first place. I assumed that within three years in the business, I would join the likes of Lawrence Kasdan and John Hughes, and be one of those Hollywood greats whose brief stint in advertising would be nothing more than a footnote in an illustrious writing career.

This was 1989, and so I got my hands on a well-known book at the time that advised college graduates on how to break into the business. It seemed easy enough. Write a few puns. Draw a few stick figures. How hard could it be? Little did I realize that the book with all its stick figures was already an outdated relic, and that I was now competing with aspiring copywriters coming out of some new school in Atlanta called Portfolio Center who had print campaigns that were not only more conceptual than mine, but that were also adorned with two-inch black borders and thirty mil lamination complete with soft felt backing. (Thank you, Mr. Laminate.)

My first interview was a disaster. My brother's girl friend had a dental hygienist who knew a Creative Director at Leo Burnett. I felt confident this was enough of a connection to call him. I mistakenly called on Yom Kippur, the holiest of all Jewish holidays and not only did I get through, but he actually agreed to meet with me. I was in. I was already anticipating the job offer and giving significant thought to which colorful tie I could wear on my first day of work to look more like Michael & Elliot from the TV show "Thirtysomething."

"You read the book with the stick figures, didn't you?" the Creative Director asked after rifling through my portfolio in less than three minutes.

"I did," I said proudly.

"Well, I'm going to save you some time. Your book is awful. Even if everyone tells you it's good, it's not."

He then gave me three tips. He told me to take a night class at Ad Ed. He suggested I read The One Show and Communication Arts.

"And whatever you do," he said, "throw out that book with the stick figures."

I took the class, got my hands on a few One Show annuals and started to fall in love with advertising. Suddenly it wasn't just a vehicle for more meaningful writing, but an art form all its own. There was real "genius" out there in the form of ads, most of it coming from some agency I'd never heard of in Minneapolis called Fallon McElligott. Their headlines were brilliant. These weren't puns. These were double entendres.

I memorized all the formulas from The One Show and put together my new and improved portfolio. My lead campaign was for Bigsby & Kruther's men's clothing store in Chicago. The first ad was a hand drawn picture of Superman's suit hanging in a closet accompanied by the headline "A successful career starts with the right suit." To round out the campaign, I had two companion pieces. One was a drawing of a space suit hanging in a closet accompanied by the line "The right suit will take you far." The third was a drawing of a priest's suit hanging in a closet accompanied by the headline "The right suit will impress the boss."

Oh, how cutting edge I was! I wasn't just selling men's suits, I was writing social commentary about religion. Who needed playwriting and screenwriting? I had my ads.

The problem was that my ads weren't working. One year after graduating from the University of Michigan, I was still waiting tables at Bennigan's. The closest I'd gotten to an advertising job offer was taking a lunch order from the Creative Recruiter at Ogilvy & Mather and having to comp her meal because I hadn't served her within the allotted fifteen minutes promised by Bennigan's Express Lunch.

Finally, my phone rang. It was a Creative Director from BBDO Chicago calling to offer me a job. "I'll take it!" I shouted before she even had a chance to tell me about the $20,000 a year salary.

BBDO Chicago had not been on my A-list of agencies. It was no Fallon. It was no Goodby. It wasn't even Eisaman Johns & Laws or Zechman & Associates, the hot boutique shops in Chicago at the time. But those agencies had all turned me down. I knew I had to get into the game somewhere. And I knew I would be an inept bartender if I stayed at Bennigan's and climbed the ranks there.

"So what if BBDO wasn't a great agency," I told myself. "I would be the one to make it great."

It was with those high hopes that I sat in my first creative briefing. It was for Doublemint Gum. Or maybe it was for Big Red. Possibly Juicy Fruit. Might have been Freedent. All I remember is that it was for one of the Wrigley Chewing Gums and Wrigley was BBDO's primary account. The agency was actually located in the Wrigley Building. This had to be a pretty important assignment they had put me on along with those seven other teams.

I walked out of the briefing bursting with ideas when the junior account person cornered me in the hall and handed me a ¾ inch tape cassette.

"What's this?" I asked.

"It's the Wrigley Brand Guidelines Video," she said. "It tells you everything you need to know about how to make a successful Wrigley Chewing Gum commercial."

I raced to the 32-inch Sony Trinitron and began watching, not quite knowing what I was in for.

The video explained that every Wrigley commercial, no matter what brand it was for, needed to follow certain rules.

Each commercial had to show a close-up of the stick of gum perfectly rounding in half as it entered someone's mouth. And that shot had to be followed by a shot of the "surprising look of satisfaction" on the gum chewer's face as he or she was hit with that burst of Wrigley Chewing Gum's superior "flavor." Or was it superior "taste?" I don't remember which word was used, but I do remember there being a long argument at the briefing over what word would best resonate emotionally with gum chewing consumers.

"I have to put these in every ad?" I asked the account person.

"Yep," she said "It's the Bite & Smile."

The Bite & Smile? Nobody had said anything about a Bite & Smile in my advertising class. I certainly hadn't seen any in The One Show. Even that book with the stick figures hadn't mentioned it.

I trudged off to my office wondering if it was too late to apply to film school. Then I sat at my desk a little older, a little wiser and a little closer to death. I had gotten my first glimpse inside the true secret to staying sane in the advertising business.

Give the clients their Bite & Smile. And in return, they'll give you an all expense paid three-week vacation at Shutters on The Beach.

Matt Eastwood
Chief Creative Officer, DDB, New York

Matt Eastwood was described by Britain's *Campaign* magazine as a "unicorn" in the communications industry. Having overseen some of the most innovative and recognisable creative projects in advertising today, his ability to guide an integrated agency vision across multiple and surprising media outlets establishes him as a star in the advertising world. His career has spanned numerous agencies, specialties and countries. Beginning with stints in Sydney at DDB as copywriter and then onto Saatchi & Saatchi as Creative Group Head. Matt quickly excelled to become a partner and founding Creative Director of M&C Saatchi Melbourne in 1996. Under his creative direction, the agency went on to be named Agency of the Year a record four years running. In 2001, Maurice Saatchi caused a stir in Britain by installing Matt "an Australian" as Executive Creative Director of his newly established M&C Saatchi London. Then, in 2003, he went on to be appointed Chairman and Executive Creative Director of M&C Saatchi New York. Settled into North America, Matt then joined Y&R as Chief Creative Officer in 2004.With home beckoning, Matt re-joined DDB Sydney in early 2006 as National Creative Director and Vice Chairman. Within 18 months, Matt's guidance resulted in DDB winning the coveted *Campaign Brief* Agency of the Year title. Whilst the following year he also added *AdNews* NSW and National Agency of the Year titles, as well as *Australian Creative* Hotshop to his ever growing list of awards. From Cannes to One Show to D&AD, the awards list is impressive. Now firmly ensconced back in the United States, Matt works on Madison Avenue and dreams about spending weekends at his lake house two and a half hours north of New York.

Matt Eastwood, My Thoughts

I only met Matt recently, through the introduction of his brother DDB CCO, Jeremy Craigen, in London; who's also a great contributor to MFT.

I'd already heard about Matt through other mutual friends; about his Australian openness and good humor and his willingness to rally the bloodied troops and lead them into the bright, white light of client acclaim. Was this guy a CCO or a four-star general?

And when we met in his office, all the info was proved true.

First, Matt greeted me with a big, warm smile and a firm handshake; all under a trim, tuxedo jacket. There were no tuxedo trousers. Just the jacket. Over a tee. So it was the old, foxy tux-over-tee trick. It won me over right away.

Besides winning tons of awards for his work down under and over here, Matt continues to love what he does. Each new brief breathes challenge. Each new idea from his creatives is reason to celebrate. Each new pitch is a mano a mano encounter to be bested. He lives for this stuff. He's done it on three continents. So far. With Matt, CCO should stand for Chief Continent Officer.

But as he told me over coffee that morning, he also loves leaving the trenches in Manhattan and retreating to the wilds upstate. He's a native Australian, I'm a native New Yorker, and I know exactly how he feels.

My First Time
By Matt Eastwood

As a young creative, I was lucky enough to be working for Ogilvy & Mather who, at the time, was Agency of the Year for the second year running. Although, I was also unlucky in that it happened to be one of Ogilvy's smallest offices, JMA/Ogilvy & Mather in Perth, Western Australia.

Those people that know Perth, know that it is one of the most isolated cities in the world. And, as you can imagine, it has production budgets to match. The craft services budget on my last shoot in New York was probably bigger than the entire budget of my first TV spot. Or, more accurately, spots. There were two of them. Which was entirely my fault.

My art director and I had written two spots for a local airline, Ansett WA. The idea was that the client would choose one. The first spot was based on the idea that the airline would treat every passenger like their only passenger. Basically, we'd see a passenger being fussed over by a hostess and when the camera pulled back we'd reveal that his seat was the only seat in the plane. The second spot would have a wife telling her kids that Dad would be tired and hungry when he got off the plane. This would be intercut with him absolutely living it up, looking anything but tired and hungry. He'd then exit the plane looking perfect. But, of course, he still wanted the sympathy of his family, so just before he exited he'd mess up his hair, ruffle his clothing and put on his best hang-dog face. Awwwh, you poor darling.

When we went to sell the ideas to the client, he chose the "Only Passenger" spot. Which would have been fine, except that I was convinced the other spot would be better. An award-winner, as I said to him.

After much a cajoling, he agreed to make both spots. I was thrilled. But only if we could do it for the original budget. Shit. The budget was $60,000. For both. This was Perth, remember, so I was used to small budgets. But, even in Perth, $60,000 for two spots is ridiculous.

But I was about to learn my first lesson. Great scripts cost less to produce. If you've got a great script, production companies are more willing to invest their own money in making it. And that's what happened. Thankfully, Terry Stone, an award-winning film director from London, had decided he'd rather live in the most isolated city in the world. Go figure. Terry loved the scripts and agreed to make them both for $60,000. At least I was no longer the biggest fool involved in the job.

The actual shoot itself was an impossible undertaking. We couldn't afford to build a set, so we had to film on an actual plane. And, because it was an actual plane, we could only get access at night. Starting at 11pm, we had to take every seat out of a Boeing 747, shoot the first spot, then put all the seats back to shoot the second spot. Worse, we had to be finished by 8am so the plane could take off the next morning.

Luckily, because this was an actual plane, the only people who could take the seats out were union workers, and union workers are known for being notoriously fast. Needless to say, by 4am, and with 4 hours to go, we still didn't have the seats back in. And we hadn't even started shooting the second spot. The so-called award-winning spot.

At 5am, with only half the seats back in, we decided to start shooting. I was learning a lot. Fast. Like that the 1st AD is the one that does all the really hard work. And that, at 5am in the morning, he's the only one that will be truly honest with you. We were not going to make it. But we kept shooting. We got some great stuff. And, even though we didn't finish on time, the plane was only an hour late taking off. Of course, it's important to note that the one hour delay probably cost the client more than the entire shoot. But, hey, they got their ad. And I got mine.

As I'd promised, the spot went on to win "Commercial of the Year" at the Perth Art Director's Club Awards. But, this exciting accolade was tempered by the fact that in the months that followed the shoot JMA/Ogilvy & Mather had gone into Chapter 11 and I'd been made redundant. So, although I accepted the biggest award of my career so far, I now had no career to speak of. Gold trophies are great, but they don't pay the rent.

However, as fate would have it, one of the show's judges was Chief Creative Officer of a hugely awarded Sydney agency, and was in the audience that night. He offered me a job then and there. Within a couple of months I had moved to Sydney and was again working at an award-winning agency. My first

TV spot carried far more significance than I could ever have known. It taught me to fight for what you believe in. And to treat every spot like it might be your last.

Because it very well might be.

Mark Fitzloff
Partner, Co-Executive Creative Director, Wieden+Kennedy Portland

Mark Fitzloff was born in Wisconsin and lived there just long enough to claim Midwestern roots before moving to the West Coast, where he belonged.

Mark came to Wieden+Kennedy as a copywriter in 1999, doing award-winning work for AltaVista and Nike. But it was while working on Coca-Cola that he found his true talent, breathing fresh life into old, iconic American brands and reminding us what we love about them.

This talent served him especially well as creative director on Old Spice. Charged with reinvigorating your grandfather's deodorant, Mark turned the brand's perceived weakness of being *old* into its primary asset, *experience*. The result has been some of the best work to come out of the Portland office in years and a steady increase in sales for the brand.

Mark brings an unusual combination of business savvy and creative thinking to the job. His ability to lead work that both wins awards and pushes the client's bottom line has served him well in the ECD role, both in impacting brands like Levi's, Target, Nike, Chrysler and P&G, and in managing the rapid growth of W+K's Portland office of 550+ people. Mark and his wife, Courtney, have a son named Max and a daughter named Mia.

Mark Fitzloff, My Thoughts

Mark isn't just the kind of guy you want to have a drink with. He's the kind of guy you want to drink.

I've known Mark since he was knee-high to a grasshopper, as the old-time cowboys' sidekicks used to say. But since I'm not an old-time cowboy sidekick, let's just say I've known Mark for over ten years.

It began with me trying to recruit him out of Wieden & Kennedy for a more senior position with substantially more financial rewards. But Mark was happy. He was staying put.

I watched as Mark created, or helped create, some of the most well-known campaigns of the last decade. Like Coca-Cola, Powerade, and all the new Old Spice spicing up the spectrum.

So once again I called Mark to recruit him out of Wieden & Kennedy for a more senior position with substantially more financial rewards. But Mark was happy. He was staying put.

This went on for more than a decade. Me, like Mephistopheles offering him untold riches, and Mark, always the gentlemen saying something akin to: Devil be gone! As if this was some sort of goddamn exorcism or something.

And where has all that slap happy crappy stuff gotten him? Fine. Yes. He's the Co-ECD/Partner of Wieden & Kennedy, Portland, one of the top creative agencies in the world

And very, very happy.

My First Time
By Mark Fitzloff

Before I ever made a TV commercial, I made everything else in advertising. I worked as an account guy; I wrote direct mail; I wrote for print and radio; I even wrote some of the very first commercial websites and banners on the Internet.

Then, six years after I started in this business, I made my first TV spot.

It was 1999. I was a brand-new copywriter working at Wieden+Kennedy in Portland on the Microsoft account. Bob Moore hired me under the assumption that I knew more about technology than your typical Wieden copywriter. That wasn't actually true, but I wasn't in a position to correct him. My book was woefully inadequate for such a place. If they wanted me to be the tech guy at W+K, then the tech guy I would be.

Then, right after I was hired, Microsoft fired the agency. I suddenly felt totally outclassed and unnecessary in a super-competitive creative department populated with folks like Jeff Kling, Jimmy Smith, Mike Folino, Jeff Williams, Ian Reichenthal, Scott Vitrone, Jeff Labbe, Monica Taylor and Derek Barnes, not to mention CDs like Jim Riswold, Chuck McBride and, um, Dan Wieden.

But I survived the layoffs. Maybe someone thought it would be too cruel to fire someone so new he still lived in corporate housing. Whatever the reason, I survived, and got moved onto the Coca-Cola business, and that's how James Selman and I got the assignment to make Coke commercials for the 2000 Summer Olympics.

Bob Moore and Todd Waterbury were our creative directors. At the time, Coke was big on a thing they called "intrinsics"—as in, the intrinsic qualities of their product. The CDs explained how the commercials needed to communicate these intrinsics, even though the taste of Coca-Cola has always been famously difficult to describe. It's not chocolaty or fruity or citrusy or anything else. It's "Coke-y." After rounds and rounds of work proving how difficult that brief was, we were allowed to shift our focus to sport. As long as we could incorporate the product in a way that made it integral to the story, we'd be fine.

Neither James nor I were big sports fans (a source of anxiety in an agency dominated by Nike), but we were both into the Olympics. James was an amazing cyclist (he would later become known for his fantastic work with Lance Armstrong), and I played water polo in college.

So we started with what we knew. We threw out interesting visual stories about our respective sports that would also manage to incorporate Coca-Cola. I had one about a bunch of Eastern Bloc oil workers watching their national team play on TV, while stationed on a drilling platform somewhere in the North Sea. While drinking Cokes and watching the game, they get the idea to throw a waterpolo ball out into the water and have a pickup game. James had an idea about a peloton of bicycle commuters in Beijing who fall into line behind a Coke delivery truck. The driver gets the idea to start passing out bottles of Coke like he's part of the support team at the Tour de France. All told we probably had about a dozen scripts, each in this "Mentos" vein, where somebody just conveniently gets an idea to do something playful or mischievous after consuming the product and then visual fun and hilarity ensue. (A cliché ad construct if ever there was one.)

In the end the client only approved one spot for production— James' cycling script. But I didn't care; we had made it to the promised land of production, and I might actually be headed to *China* to make my first TV spot.

But then politics got in the way. Not office politics, but actual politics. Back in those days, it was still very difficult to produce commercials in Communist China. So the client wondered if we could produce the spot in LA. Well, okay. Not quite as exotic, but still, production! Then Coke decided that since this was a global spot, it had to take place in a global (vs. a North American) location. Okay! Back to getting that passport. Then they figured that since the Olympics would be happening in Sydney, the spot should shoot in Sydney. More Okay! But in the end, Australia also presented logistical problems, so the location ended up being New Zealand. That's right, I shot my very-first-ever-TV commercial in Middle-earth. Way before Peter Jackson and his Hobbits got there.

I imagine I must've still been in a daze when I boarded the plane for Auckland. Not only was I leaving for New Fucking Zealand for my first-ever TV shoot, but I was leaving on my first-ever business class flight, since at the time it was agency policy to fly business-class overseas. Accompanying me on the flight were Mr. Selman, an account executive named Jessica Hoffman and a producer named Robyn Boardman. The first person we met off the plane was our director, Johan Renck.

In the universe of the highly impressionable junior copywriter, there is no shinier star than the commercial director. Johan was the first one I'd ever met and he was perfectly cast, a big blond Swede (of course) with ironic mullet/Beckham hair. He also happened to be a moderately famous pop star in Europe called Stakka Bo.[1]

When you go on a long production, you really develop a strong bond with the people you're working with. The distance we had to travel for this one made this particularly true, and it soon became apparent that Johan would be our team leader. The other team members included Johan's line producer, his DP and a PA from the local production company who would be our driver for the two-week stay.

The phase just prior to rolling film is called preproduction; it's when you cast actors, nail down locations, secure permits and build props, and it culminates in an important client meeting called the "pre-pro." This is when clients and agency folks get to give the final sign-off on all sorts of decisions or forever hold their peace. For that reason, it can also be the most stressful part of the entire process. As testament to that, our creative director, Todd Waterbury, flew all the way to New Zealand from Portland just to attend the meeting in person, flying home the very next day. This left quite an impression on me. I admired Todd's commitment to the job, but I was also sort of shocked that he considered the client meeting the only part of the shoot worth his attention. I was so naïve. Pre-pros are really where spots get made. If they go well, and if all the hard conversations happen up-front, everything else just falls into place. But at this point, I was under the Svengali sway of Stakka Bo, and to us Todd was just *the man from headquarters* sent to check up on us. Meanwhile I was busy learning to appreciate the finer things in life under the tutelage of my

---

[1] An interesting side-note: when the music video for Stakka Bo's hit single "Here We Go" appeared on a 1994 episode of Beavis and Butt-Head, Beavis responded to it by saying "this new Ace of Base song sucks."

director. Things like New Zealand Bluff oysters, world renowned for their succulence and flavor, but only in season for two weeks out of the year. Johan had made it his mission to ingest nothing but Bluff oysters and French champagne for the duration of the shoot. I was attempting to keep pace with him, and did so until my stomach decided otherwise.

The shoot was a massive production. Streets were closed off, special vehicles were rigged with cameras and a cast of several dozen extras was dispersed throughout the scenes. The scale of that shoot has always stuck with me. This was when I learned how many people it takes to actually pull off a TV commercial. I poured myself into the educational experience, studying the pre-pro book, trying to figure out who the gaffer was, and how he differed from the grip (FYI the former manages electrical, while the latter deals with camera rigging), what the 1st AD did, compared to the 2nd AD (among other things, the 1st manages the on camera set, while the 2nd oversees the backstage and off-camera work). It was a great shoot to learn on because all the crew disciplines were represented. In the midst of it all, I walked around feeling important, the creator of the idea! The reason why all of us were there! In reality I was without a doubt, the single least important person on the entire set.

After the shoot, we flew back to Portland to edit. I remember sharing the rough cut with Jim Riswold. In my presentation to him, he told me he hated the spot, and thought it was possibly the worst piece of creative the agency had done all year. That may have been a (slight) exaggeration, but the spot certainly wasn't anything special by W+K standards. Let's just say it left me lots of room to improve upon my craft.

Despite the outcome, the project was an amazing experience that I'm still thankful for. It ingrained in me a belief that execution is just as important as "the big idea," which I think is a hallmark of W+K work. I also fell in love with my job on that shoot: the thrill of making something, the camaraderie of production and, of course the exotic travel. Although, in my 13 years of making TV commercials, I still haven't traveled abroad for another shoot!

Here's the spot if you'd like to see it: http://vimeo.com/4862481

Ian Grais
Founder, ECD, Rethink Canada

Ian Grais was born and raised in Western Canada. He studied Economics at the University of British Columbia then advertising and design at the Art Center College of Design in Pasadena, prior to founding Rethink in 1999.

At Rethink Ian creates and directs a wide range of projects encompassing design, interactive, installation and advertising. Ian has been ranked by Strategy Magazine as the number one art director and creative director in Canada for the past decade.

Currently Ian serves on The Graphic Design Advisory Committee at Kwantlen Polytechnic University and Langara College as well as the Professional Advisory Board for the Illustration program at Sheridan College in Ontario.

.

Ian Grais, My Thoughts

Until I read Ian's story, I had no idea that the first time I tried to recruit him, he was only eight years into his advertisinghood. I had seen his work, thought it was incredible, and contacted him about an important position.

Ian was interested, but had to check with the boss, his wife. It seemed that she wasn't overly excited about the location and that nixed that.

The next time I contacted Ian, his wife was interested but he really wasn't.

Hmmmm. Perhaps I could arrange a divorce. Nah, not nice. Back to the drawingboard.

By the time I got around to calling Ian again, he had launched his own agency, Rethink/Canada, and was on his way to having me trying to find people (and their significant others) for him in Vancouvover. And this was way before the Olympics.

If you're Canadian, this is a jackpot. Vancouver is so beautiful and cosmopolitan. If you're an American, it's like: "Vancouver? What are you nuts? They got ice and Innuits, Innuits and ice; go to hell". Or some such nice declarative sentence.

But Ian has been so successful that he's opened an office in Toronto, too. So now I have *two* cities Americans know nothing about.
Oh, well.

*A special note on Ian's stories. Yes, I said stories. When Ian wrote to me, he said he was breaking the rule, that he had two stories, one from his school; and could I please include this, as well, as he thought it more interesting for you to read about one of our people's experiences in ad school. And he was right. I hope your experiences were as good.

My First Time
By Ian Grais

I want to share two firsts with you. My first officially produced ads, if you don't include the tens of posters my parents had me produce by hand for various church bazaars and bake sales. And my first "Aha!" moment, when I knew I could do this thing called "art direction".

It happened at Art Center College of Design in Pasadena, fall semester 1990. I was 23 in my second year of the Advertising program. The class was a required credit called Visual Communication taught by Lou Danziger. Lou was known at the time as one of the very best Art Center teachers, having been a contemporary of Paul Rand and having had a legendary career in graphic design. He also possessed an enormous knowledge (and library) of the history of graphic design, which he taught to the whole school. Needless to say, this was an intimidating class.

We weren't creating advertising in the class, to the chagrin of many attending: Lou had us working on the fundamentals. At the time he didn't differentiate between graphic design and advertising solutions, he taught us that it was all visual communication and so we needed to communicate clearly in an original way. His famous question was "what are you trying to say?" Which he repeated over and over.

He taught us that to answer this we needed to find what's unique about the communication problem we're trying to solve. Every problem is unique, we learned, and if we could find a custom solution to our particular problem then our solution was sure to be original. He reminded us that the 'form' can be found inside the 'in**form**ation'.

So each class was given simple visual problems which we needed to solve, problems like: communicate 'loud" without using words. We'd lean our 8 ½" x 11" mounted solutions on the critique rails in class and wait our turn as Lou did his rounds giving us critique and advice, as the class discussed what they saw.

One of the problems we all had was that our solutions were not very clear, and if they were clear they weren't very specific. Lou would carefully articulate the flaws in each solution, emphasizing all the ambiguities present in our work. We were learning to be objective about our work and that others don't always see what we as creators see.

Lou used an analogy of a hallway with many doors, where our job was to get someone to enter only one of the doors. He asked us how we'd accomplish this and we suggested putting signs on the doors or arrows on the floor for the person to follow. Lou's solution didn't leave any room for chance; he said the only way to be sure that they'll only go through the door you want them to, is to lock all of the other doors.

One of our assignments was to create a new symbol for Christmas. I remember thinking long and hard about this problem as I jotted down all of the usual symbols like holly, bells, elves, etc. I wasn't creating anything new and I kept coming back to overused clichés. Which struck me is exactly the problem with Christmas: it's lost its charm because it's been totally commercialized. Suddenly I had a point of view and an idea: use a UPC code to make a simple Christmas tree, letting the code numbers be the date. I wasn't sure what Lou would think but I knew I was saying something truthful with this solution.

So I carefully cut a UPC code and set the type, then mounted the small symbol and put it up on the rail with everyone else's homework and waited nervously for my "crit".

When Lou came to my solution he wasn't shy, he loved it, which took the whole class by surprise; I think because he hadn't reacted this enthusiastically before.

Suddenly I felt like I had made magic and I experienced how a "flash" of inspiration can solve a specific problem. This gave me confidence in my process and taught me that following my instincts pays off. It also led to me getting a private study with Lou where I was fortunate to learn one-on-one with a great master. To this day I try to solve every problem I face at Rethink with discipline learned by these classes. Thanks Lou!

My first actual ads that I produced were for the popular LA Weekly newspaper. At the time, I was still a student at Art Center and spending a lot of time with a friend named Kim Watt, one of the only people I knew in LA who was also from Vancouver. Kim was working for the LA Weekly and knew that they wanted to run some billboards, so she asked me if I was interested. Interested?! I was dieing to have a real client and couldn't believe my luck. I had no idea how to even start a client relationship, so I just trusted Kim to give me the brief.

Sure enough they had some contra media they wanted to use and didn't have any creative to run, so they were willing to give a student a try. I was only mid-way through my courses so I didn't even have a proper advertising portfolio yet. I was given this opportunity without review as a long shot. I guess all of my passionately told stories to Kim about Art Center's rigorous Instruction gave her the impression that I could do a better job than their in-house designers. Thanks for believing Kim!

I remember going to the presentation with just one idea to recommend. I had developed a lot of options but was very confident in my recommended idea. It was the one, I knew it, and nobody was going to tell me differently. When I presented my comps to the renowned editor at the time, Jay Levin, he was pensive and very quiet. He liked the concept but had his own ideas about the phrases I had chosen. He also had colour suggestions. I remember him suggesting the phrase "No Placebos" which I delicately tried to counter by suggesting that not everyone would understand this (because I didn't understand it).

I remember leaving the meeting feeling kind of defeated because the client didn't accept my work as perfect and approve it exactly as presented on the spot. I didn't know what compromise felt like so I didn't know how to react.

Looking back I had far too much ego for my little bit of experience. The good news was that the client actually wanted to produce the ads so I was tasked with getting them final art, selecting new colours and working through production. This was very exciting and it seamed like forever before I was told of the nine (!) locations that my work would appear. When I saw the finished product I was oh so proud and also scared that my classmates would disapprove because the ads weren't exactly how I had envisioned them.

As it turned out everyone was impressed and the ads got a modest, positive response. I didn't know what to expect as a follow up and was a little disappointed when nothing at all happened. The boards came and went and for a brief time I could say that "yeah I was the guy who did those billboards on Melrose".

My first real taste of advertising fame! (pictured)

R. Vann Graves
EVP, Executive Creative Director, McCann Worldgroup, NY

Vann joined McCann Worldgroup's New York office in 2009 where he quickly became a contributor to the agency's key accounts, including MasterCard, U.S. Army and General Mills. He was promoted in 2011 to Executive Creative Director and currently he runs the US Army and American Airlines Accounts.

Prior to joining McCann, Vann was Chief Creative Officer of UniWorld Group, where he oversaw the agency's work for clients such as 3 Musketeers, Ford Motor company, Home Depot, Time Warner Cable and U.S. Marine Corps. He began his career at BBDO New York where he worked for 15 years, creating advertising for brands such as Visa, AT&T, Gillette, M&Ms, and Motorola.

Vann has explored the world, for business, fun and even war. A decorated combat veteran, Vann took a leave of absence from his agency career after 9/11 to join the U.S. Army.

Vann's work has earned numerous creative honors. He has the distinction of being named a Fulbright Senior Specialist. He is a former co-Chair on the executive board for the 4A's MAIP Alumni Program, The Board of Trustees for the Pratt Institute, and the Adversity Board for The One Club. Vann holds a BBA from Howard University, a MS from the Pratt Institute. Challenged by financing his own education, he established an endowed scholarship for students interested in a career in advertising. He is married to Autumn A. Graves, president of Girard College in Philadelphia.

Van Graves, My Thoughts

With Vann, where do I begin?

I first contacted him about a very funny Snickers commercial he had done; that was back in 2001. And we've remained friends ever since.

When I first met him, I came home and told my wife that Vann is the kind of young man you just don't meet anymore. Talented, respectful. There was something with Vann that was just different. And he proved me more than right. Like you wouldn't believe.

Here's the story; but as I said, you may not believe it.

After 9/11, Vann, who had a great job in a great agency, BBDO/New York, not too far from where 9/11 happened, enlisted in the Army and went to Ft. Jackson, SC for training. The guy enlisted!

Then he was shipped to Iraq where he served his country bravely and, thankfully, came home safe and sound and ready to fight different battles.

And while there were no IEDs at BBDO, there were account execs and planners, and clients. Suddenly Iraq didn't seem like such a bad place.

After a while he moved on to become ECD at McCann for, what else, the Army? How cool and perfect and right is that?

To me, Vann represents the best of what the American ad world, and America as a whole, have to offer.

My First Time
R.Vann Graves

At heart I'm just a kid from Richmond, Virginia who watched way too much television growing up. So it was kind of a shock when I found myself interning at BBDO New York during grad school. After my summer internship I was kept on with the made up title of "permanent part-time assistant art director" while I finished my degree. I was then hired full time as an Assistant Art Director and eventually ended up working in Charlie Miesmer's group. This was awesome; not only was he one of the best in advertising, but his group included folks like Gerry Graf, Susan Credle and Jimmy Sieigel. I reported to Jimmy, who ran the VISA account, one of the many big brands BBDO had at the time.

Now that I actually worked at BBDO, I imagined I'd start shooting epic TV commercials in the first week or two. Unfortunately, my first spot didn't come along quite as quickly as I had hoped. As a junior creative, you always think that every idea you come up with is great and should go straight into production. However, it wasn't long until I started to understand the reason why people said that BBDO stood for *Bring it Back, Do it Over*—because that's exactly what we did, again and again... and again. BBDO was also regarded as a place where they "eat their young," especially if they didn't produce. So the pressure was on to sell something, and to sell it fast.

At the time my partner and I were involved in several projects simultaneously, including the launch of the New VISA Platinum card and coming up with a Pizza Hut spot. We worked night and day and, when we weren't working, we worried about how we'd ever get through all of the work expected of us.

One evening, I was still in the office trying to come up with ideas for the VISA campaign when my girlfriend called and asked: "Do you remember what's happening tomorrow?" Of course I had no freakin' clue what she was talking about—she of all people knew that we'd been working 24/7. However, as I fumbled frantically through my calendar, instead of coming clean I replied: "Uh, yeah, of course I do..." This was met with squeals of excitement and she started to chatter away about how excited she was that we were spending time together and how she couldn't wait to see me. I quickly excused myself from the call, saying: "It's going to be awesome, I can't wait!"

After I had hung up, it took me a while to figure out what exactly it was that she had been talking about. Then it hit me: it was our "anniversary", we had been dating for six months. She had mentioned that she never saw the *Usual Suspects*, so we met, had dinner, and then headed off to the dollar theater. To be honest, after three weeks of late nights and working weekends, I found it extremely hard to remain awake during the first part of the movie. However, I perked up as it progressed and I was especially riveted by the last moments, when Detective Kujan dropped his cup. Long after the film, Verbal Kint's words echoed in my head: "The greatest trick the devil ever pulled was convincing the world he didn't exist..."

The next morning I had an epiphany and wrote my first spot—Orient Express. It began with a scene in which a man is working late at the office and is called by his wife: "Do you know what Thursday is?" she asks. Linking my reality to the script, he has totally forgotten about their anniversary. Then, like Verbal Kint, he makes up a story about the extravagant trip he has planned, using objects in his office for the inspiration for his tale. And that was it. I shared the idea with my partner, she cleaned it up and we added it to our pile of scripts before setting off like lambs to the slaughter.

To our surprise, Jimmy loved the spot—and my partner for writing it (this had less to do with my partner and more with the fact that, at the time, BBDO was a writer's agency and that's just how things were). Regardless, I was floating—VISA was going to spend a million dollars bringing a concept I had envisaged to life... it was nuts!

As though we were on a run of good luck, the next day we also sold an idea for Pizza Hut. It was about a guy who lost Pizza Hut's delivery number because the Post-It note he had written it on was stuck to his butt. As he searched frantically through his apartment and turned his back to the screen, the viewers saw the number. This too was based on a mishap I had personally experienced when, having first met my girlfriend, I lost her number (for the record, it was stuck to my shoe, not my ass).

So after never being able to sell anything, I now had my first two spots shooting during the same week—Pizza Hut in New York and VISA in LA. Obviously I wanted to cover both of them but I didn't think I could make it happen. Phil Dusenbury, who generously lent me way more of his time than I probably deserved, told me how important it was to be there and pushed me to find a way to make it happen. Thinking through all of the logistics, I realized I *could* cover both shoots. I'd do all of the pre-production for the VISA spot in LA, fly back to New York for the Pizza Hut shoot and then head back to LA and not miss a thing.

Everything started out great—I did the prep in LA and made it back to the studio in New York about 30 minutes before the Pizza Hut shoot was due to start. After chatting with Charlie on set, we were ready to roll. The director called "action" and the actor started to look around for the number, just like we'd instructed. Then he really started to go for it. Within 30 seconds he had climbed up on chair and then on to the bookshelf. Then he fell... and didn't move. The guy was on his back and in serious pain. We were all horrified.

After the ambulance left the set, we used another actor to finish the shoot. I was still in shock when, in a strange moment of encouragement, Charlie approached me and asked me what I was still doing on set. Smiling, he warned me that I better not "fuck up" the VISA shoot. That was my cue to get moving—I headed back to LA and spent the whole flight praying that the next shoot would go better than the last one. Luckily, the VISA spot went without a hitch (or ambulance) and, because both spots turned out well, I soon got promoted to Art Director. It was great—exciting, fulfilling, amazing. What they say really is true: you never forget your first time!

Susan Hoffman
Partner, Co-Executive Creative Director, Wieden & Kennedy, Portland

One of our few Portland natives, Susan Hoffman started her career as an art director at Pihas, Schmidt, Westerdahl before moving to TBWA\Chiat\Day in Seattle. Three years later she came to Wieden+Kennedy as employee No. 8 and has spent the last 27 years defining the agency's culture and setting the bar for creative excellence. Susan has a tendency to shake things up a bit. That's probably because she finds the status quo boring. Case in point, a walk past the Dakota building in New York City inspired her choice of The Beatles song "Revolution" for the Nike spot of the same name. She's injected her unique perspective into some of the most memorable ads W+K has produced for virtually every client we've ever had. Susan is never satisfied unless the work feels fresh and interesting.

Since David Kennedy's "retirement" in 1993, Susan has provided the visual yin to Dan Wieden's storytelling yang. She's worked as a creative director, opened both our Amsterdam and London offices, serving both as executive creative director, and ran Wieden+ Kennedy 12, our experimental ad school. Along the way she's introduced the world to directors like David Fincher and Michael Bay and helped launch the careers of many of the most successful creative directors in the industry. In her current role as executive creative director of the flagship office, she's tasked with preserving what makes this agency special, continuing to nurture the creative talent within our walls and pushing forward to find new and different ways of working and thinking.

Susan Hoffman, My Thoughts

Susan Hoffman must feel like taffy – people pulling at her in every conceivable direction. I won't say she's busy, but being one of the most senior creative women in the world, you have to set up a meeting six months in advance to set up a meeting six months in advance.

Susan and I had never spoken before MFT, so I asked Mark Fitzloff for the introduction, and Mark, being one of the kindest people on the planet happily agreed, but said: "You know it'll take me months just to speak with her?"

Finally, the six months had come and gone and I was about to speak with Susan. It went like this:

Me: Susan, it's great to finally speak with you.
Susan: Yes it is.
Me: Mark said you'd be OK with writing your story about your first commercial.
Susan: You believe in the tooth fairy, too?
Me: I believe Mark. And he wrote a great story.
Susan: Has he sold you that bridge in Brooklyn, yet? What could that jerk possibly write about?
Me: He wrote a very funny story about his first shoot.
Susan: He lies like a rug. But fine, I'll do it. It'll take me six months but I'll do it.

And she did.
And it took six months.

My First Time
By Susan Hoffman

My first commercial was for NIKE. It was called "The Shooter", for boys' basketball shoes. I was the art director and Jim Riswold was the writer.

I naively remember when we sent the boards out, how excited all the production companies were about the idea. Now realizing they just wanted the work, good or bad.

We were clueless if it was good or not, but it made us feel great.

So we had an approved concept, hired the director, and headed to LA for the shoot.

But when we arrived for the pre-pro, we found out the idea had already been done.

Our creative directors were Dan and David and they said we needed to quickly re-concept the spot because the airdates couldn't change and we had to stick with the shoot schedule.

So we walled ourselves up in our depressing hotel room and called Dan/David every hour with new ideas (mind you this was back in 1985 when even fax machines weren't invented!).

And in the early years of WK we didn't stay at nice hotels. We stayed at this dump off of Franklin that was so bad, that on another shoot for Kink Radio, the client called me and said she was too scared to stay in the hotel. So it wasn't like Jim and I were sitting by the pool lapping up the sun as we merrily re-concepted.

I just emailed Jim and asked him the name of the place and I quote: "I remember getting stuck in the same room of that place with Wieden. He can snore with the best of them. In fact, he can suck the paint off the walls with his snoring. I, thankfully, cannot remember the name of the place." Oh well.

Another classic Riswold story from the shoot was that he had barely stepped out of Seattle, Washington. Portland, Oregon was a big move for him; so going to LA was like an international city. And he brought travelers checks!

So here we were walled up in the scary hotel sending ideas to Dan/David. The account person, Kelly Stout, had also flown down with us and later that day, when she saw how desperate we were, she started throwing in her own ideas.

She had one idea that we begrudgingly thought was OK, quickly called Dan/David, they approved it and that was the spot we produced. But you can't appreciate it until you see it. Probably the worst ad done at WK!

Here's the link:

http://wk.wiredrive.com/l/p/?presentation=e125edc9c5630160d0da4d1108f31285

Gerry Human
Executive Creative Director, Ogilvy & Mather, London

After 23 years of hawking ideas to famous brands like Audi, BMW, Coca Cola, Dove and Virgin Atlantic, I've learnt one thing: there is no nice, easy, compact answer when it comes to making great work.

It's a messy, complicated business.

Luckily, a lot of imaginative, resourceful and resilient people help me trudge through all the muck. Beneath which we occasionally find a little treasure.

Gerry's work has been honoured with a multitude of creative accolades, notably 44 Cannes Lions (including Gold in Film, Outdoor and Cyber) as well as 3 Grand Prix at the London International Awards.

Gerry Human, My Thoughts

Whilst on a business trip to London (must be properly British here), John O'Keeffe was kind enough to introduce me to Gerry.

When I got to Gerry's office, you could tell that, though he maintained an amazing aura of preternatural calm, the poor man was under siege by all manner of creative, account, planning, media, and tech people. I won't say the line outside his office waiting to speak with him was long, but it did stretch to Edinburgh.

Anyway, Gerry bade me seat myself, then wanted to know just who I was. It seems that he had no clue. He was just going on John's "Pip, pip, mate. You must see this chap. He's a colonial sod from the States; poor blighter." Or something like that.

So Gerry the Gentleman, which is how I shall forever refer to him, took the time to listen to what we were doing with "MFT" and, of course, how I could help him in recruiting. He loved the idea of "MFT", signed on immediately and we also began a business relationship, as well. Smart man, Gerry.

Of course while we were going through all this he kept a wary eye on the line outside, happy that his P.A. was keeping his colleagues in check with something resembling a medieval mace.

Finally, Gerry is originally from Joburg (Johannesburg) and I have many relatives there. So as I sat and listened to him tell me about his personal history, how much he loved doing what he's doing and how much he hopes to accomplish for his agency and his clients, I could hear my cousins speaking to me, as well. It was nice.

My First Time
By Gerry Human

Damn, just when I thought I'd erased it from memory.

My first fumble and grope-in-the-dark with advertising is not something I recall with too much pride or happy nostalgia.

For some time I wasn't even allowed to go near an actual ad. I was after all, Hunt Lascaris TBWA's official award-certificate hanger. Reviewing my work usually involved loping alongside John Hunt as he marched down the hallway, pointing out (and removing) imperfectly aligned frames. I was taught the value of humility long before I learned to appreciate the value of ideas.

That said, I remember my first "proper" ad rather vividly.

It was 1989. Reg Lascaris had an entrepreneur mate with an idea set to make a mint. It was a product targeted at cat lovers in Europe. Millions of feline fans had a problem in their otherwise aesthetically sensible lives: where the cat shat.

Like many European bogs, it tended to be a fairly nasty affair: a pungent assemblage of paper, cardboard and sandy stuff. Reg's mate had invented a solution for this woeful situation: a posh loo for cats, called Kitty Loo. Being a bit of an entrepreneur himself, Reg thought it was genius. So much so that he was prepared to invest by providing his advertising services for nothing.
Enter Gerry Human.

By that stage, I had graduated from the corridor to an office (the former copier room). And I even had my own writer, the talented and idiosyncratic Ms. Claire Harrison. Naturally, we grabbed the opportunity to do an actual commercial and wrote a script something like this:

Open on a stylish, contemporary kitchen. We notice a cat basket with a fluffy tail poking out.
V/o: "Cats are wonderful pets, but sometimes they can seem like a totally different animal."

A skunk emerges from the cat basket.
V/o: "Now there's Kitty Loo."
The skunk looks around, spots the Kitty Loo and goes inside.
V/o: "Some stuff about how Kitty Loo worked."
The skunk emerges as a Persian cat.
Logo: Kitty Loo. (Don't remember what the clever line at the end was.)

Everyone liked it, including the wonderful humour director, David Gillard. Luckily he had done a lot of nice work for the agency, so didn't mind that we had no money. (Sound familiar?)

The shoot, however, didn't go exactly to plan. I mean, what were we thinking? We wanted a skunk to climb out of a basket, walk across a fully-lit studio kitchen, and then climb into this W weird-looking plastic contraption. Needless to say, once we got him in the basket, the skunk wasn't going anywhere.

The assistant director had a cunning plan: insert an air-blowing device underneath the basket, to encourage the critter to move on "action". Upon feeling a jet of air blown up its arse, the terrified creature leapt about 3 feet into the air, and froze. In the middle of the kitchen. The "animal trainer" then had the task of coercing the paralyzed skunk into Kitty Loo, so that its transformation into a Persian cat could occur. This actually did happen, but it took the poor beast about 2 hours to crawl across the room.

The Persian cat on the other hand, couldn't be arsed to go anywhere near the Kitty Loo. Especially after it had been previously occupied by a properly smelly skunk.

We did eventually piece an ad together, but I don't think the product ever really made it onto the production line, let alone take Europe by storm. Needless to say, I never got to hang an award certificate for it, either. But critically, I learned a few things from the experience:

> Advertising is fun.
> When you're having fun it shows in your work.
> When advertising is entertaining, people buy products because of it. (Ok, maybe not Kitty Loos.)

That's all there is to it, really.

Maxi Itzkoff

Co-ECD, Del Campo Nazca Saatchi & Saatchi

Maxi Itzkoff, along with his partner, Mariano Serkin, are the most awarded creatives in Argentina. For the past five years, he has been Executive Creative Director at Del Campo Saatchi&Saatchi Buenos Aires, the #1 agency in Argentina and one of the top 5 agencies worldwide.

Maxi began his career very early, at the age of 19, starting out as a copywriter at Lowe Agulla & Baccetti in Buenos Aires, the agency that revolutionized advertising in Argentina. He has also worked in Europe, spending time at DDB London, BBDO Spain, and Publicis Lado C Spain, a creative boutique created to handle Renault account. During his career Maxi has worked for such important global clients as P&G, Renault, Cadbury, PlayStation, Sony Cybershot, InBev (Norte-Andes), Coca-Cola, Sprite, Burger King, Adidas, BGH home appliances, and HSBC, among others. He has won awards at all major national and international festivals, including 19 Grand Prix, one of which at Cannes for the Andes "Teletransporter" campaign (2010).   Under his leadership, Del Campo Saatchi&Saatchi has won numerous awards and accolades. It was selected "Agency of the Year" at the Circulo Argentino de Creativos in 2006, 2007, 2008, 2009, 2010, and 2011. In 2010, *Ad Age* named Del Campo Saatchi&Saatchi "International Agency of the Year", and in 2011 they named the agency "Most Creative Shop" worldwide. And in 2011, the agency was ranked #4 on the *Gunn Report.* Maxi was also named "Regional Creative Director of the Year" at El Ojo de Iberoamerica in both 2010 and 2011.

Maxi Itzkoff, My Thoughts

Of all the contributors to MFT, Maxi is the only one I haven't spoken with. Though we've tried.

We've set up times, but every time I called, I couldn't get through. It really was "Don't Cry For Me, Argentina, Just Let Me Speak With Maxi". It was odd since Mariano, his CO-ECD, and I had spoken numerous times.

I know Maxi exists. Mariano told me so. And Maxi sent me his picture, and his story, and hey, wait a minute, what if there really is no Maxi? What if Mariano has created an ECD partner, wrote this story and wants me and everyone else to *believe* he exists?

What kind of trickery is this? What twisted master plot by a master creative to make a Maxi and fob the faux on the world?

Nah, Mariano isn't like that. But wait. What if it's Maxi who created a faux Mariano, and it's been Maxi, as Mariano, who's been speaking with me and sending me all the stories? What twisted maser plot by a master creative to make a Mariano and fob the faux on the world?

I just gave myself a huge headache and I need to lie down.

My First Time
By Maxi Itzkoff

Fortunately or unfortunately, I began my career in advertising very young. I was 19 years old.

At that time I didn't really understand what the ad industry was all about. And maybe that was a good thing because if I had known how much I'd have to suffer before I could finally create good work, I probably would have followed the other career path I was considering – engineering.

As a kid, I was fascinated by everything related to technology. I had an innate ability to create inventions without any previous study, a trait I probably inherited from my father, who was an engineer.

When I was 10 years old I began building remote control cars. I also had a habit of dissecting electrical components around the house and using them to build new ones. I was crazy about technology, but what I was truly passionate about was provoking others with my inventions.

When I was 14 I designed a sort of installation in my room using lights, sounds, and images, which was powered by a remote control. It terrified everyone who came in.

I tell this story because it defines exactly the sort of work that I wanted to develop professionally.

Perhaps this is why it was so difficult for me to do my first print ad.

From my perspective, the print ads that always won at festivals were only good according to the judges' standards. But consumers didn't understand them. They weren't provocative in the slightest. I wanted to find something that would appeal to both targets- the actual public, as well as advertisers. I was searching for a way to make my work real and provocative.

In 1999, at the second agency I worked for, "Agulla&Baccetti" (the agency that revolutionized advertising in Argentina), I was lucky enough to work for Burger King.

As it was a small account at the time, I was put in charge. Oddly enough, I didn't even eat hamburgers. Obviously, the client was less than thrilled to hear this. To quell their hesitations and to get a better understanding of the product, I decided to work on the campaign every day directly from a Burger King restaurant.

The brief was very clear: we had to express that Burger King burgers were bigger than the competition's (McDonald's), as well as the fact that they were grilled. The problem was that McDonald's had about 1,000 restaurants in Argentina, whereas Burger King only had 15. This was also reflected in their budget. Burger King didn't have the resources for a massive media campaign. But what they did have were bigger, tastier hamburgers.

So we spent a few weeks thinking. I'll never forget this ad because it put my job on the line.

The creative directors were at Cannes at the time. And I decided that instead of calling them, I would take responsibility for the first ad that the agency was going to create for the brand.

This was an agency that didn't allow second chances. One bad ad and you were out.

Burger King had arranged to have a huge billboard placed right above one of their restaurants that was strategically located in an area of Buenos Aires where thousands of people passed by every day. Surprisingly, this particular Burger King was sandwiched between two McDonald's restaurants.

Using this to our advantage, we created one of the most buzzed-about billboards at a time when social networks didn't exist. It was on the cover of newspapers and a topic of conversation on radio and television.

McDonald's contacted the agency asking us to drop Burger King and start working for them for five times the money. The agency obviously declined on principal.

It became more than just a billboard- it was a point of interest for people passing by. They returned again and again to see the latest billboard and find out how the story of the ad would unfold.

Eight months later, I was working for a short time at DDB London (I had decided to spend my vacations working at an agency outside the country). I received a phone call from Buenos Aires. It was the ECD of the agency in Argentina. He gave me the first incredible news of my career: "You've won your first Clio, and it's a gold."

This was the ad:

The poster was placed above Burger King, between two McDonald's restaurants.

Chris Jacobs
Executive Creative Director,Cramer-Krasselt,Milwuakee

Chris leads the work on over 35 different brands – from Seadoo and Skidoo to Pyrex to Spice Islands. Before joining Cramer-Krasselt, Chris was SVP, Creative Director at The Martin Agency.

Over his career, Chris has won medals at every major international award show, including Cannes, The One Show, The NY Art Director's Show, The ANDY's, and the Effie's. He has also been a judge numerous award shows, including The One Show.

Chris Jacobs, My Thoughts

Chris is the kind of creative you just have to look up to. Literally. He's 6'5".

I've only known him for a few years, but I've come to know that he's absolutely one of the nicest people walking the planet. And at that height, he could probably walk the planet in a couple of days.

The first thing you hear when you speak with Chris on the phone is a soft, Southern accent that immediately puts you at ease because there's such a warmth and feeling of genuine humor there. He's won you over just by picking up the phone.

He had originally been referred to me by a mutual friend who spoke of him in terms you only hear as a eulogy. I didn't know if I'd be speaking with a candidate or a corpse.

Chris is the type of ECD you would want to interview with just so you could relax and have the tensions slip away. It's like verbal shiatsu. He's made potential creative hires so at home during these interviews that they've moved their belongings into his office without getting hired.

As you've seen from his bio, Chris had been one of the most senior creative leaders in the south when he moved to Milwaukee smack dab in the middle of winter, no less. And I believe, though I have no empirical data to substantiate this, that the Milwaukee winters suddenly became much milder than usual.

My First Time
By Chris Jacobs

The first ad I ever produced was in 1986. That would be the year that Huey Lewis, Heart, Cyndi Lauper, and Bananarama all had #1 hits. So I can't really say my career began in an era of cultural creative revolution.

I was taking part in a five day internship at The Martin Agency. I was a senior in high school, which by definition means I was an idiot. And one of the interns sitting next to me was a girl who had just graduated from Harvard. In short, I was way out of my league.

The first two days of the internship involved sitting in one meeting after another while people from media, account management, and creative all came in and said, "Here is what we do...Blah...Blah...Blah...." The people were nice, but it wasn't exactly very inspiring or fun.

But the last three days were different. You see every intern got to pick a department to go work in and do something for the remainder of the week. I mean actually "DO" something, not just sit in a chair and listen. I think most of us picked the creative department.

On that third day, I was pretty pumped up. I mean I grew up around ad agencies. My father was a creative director. And since I was a kid I had seen the raw sketches, storyboards, and marked up contact sheets lying around my house. This was my chance to go actually do what I had only ever watched from afar. So that Wednesday, the five of us interns met up with our "mentor." (Or basically the creative guy that agreed to have a bunch of kids dumped on him for three days.) And from what I heard, this guy was a big hotshot writer at the agency. He was winning the big national awards. And as soon as I met him, he appeared like he was a really creative kind of guy (he had sort of long hair and seemed real smart and edgy.)

His name was Luke Sullivan. Yeah, that guy.

One of the greatest advertising writers in the history of the business. And I think most would put him at the top of the educational leaders in the world right now when it comes to advertising. I certainly do. But this was 1986. I don't think at that time Luke had spent a lot of time "teaching." I'm guessing he was focused on building his increasingly high stack of One Show Pencils.

I remember that day sitting with the intern group at this small conference table in an empty office. And I can't speak for the other interns, but I was super excited. The assignment was coming. My first ad. The chance to create or write something.

Well, Luke walks in and he's holding a tall stack of Communication Arts Advertising annuals. And he puts them on the table right in the middle of us. And he says, "If you want to do great advertising, then read these. Memorize these books." (This was 25 years ago, so I'm not 100% sure those were his exact words. But that's how I remember it.)

And then Luke left the room. There was some silence as all of us kind of looked at each other a bit confused. I mean we were there to "DO something" - not "read something." But we were completely intimidated students, so we did as we were told. We just picked up those CA annuals and started going through them. But as students, we were used to text books and these weren't text books. Hell, there was no text explaining anything. These were just picture books. Page after page of ads. Nothing to explain why it was made or, most importantly, how they came up with that brilliant creative idea.

Then on the second day, Andy Ellis (another great writer at Martin) popped his head in the door and asked, "How's it going? What are you guys doing?" We explained the CA annuals and Luke's instructions. And Andy kind of said, "Luke, what the hell?" Then Andy left. We all worried that we just created some problem between Andy and Luke.

But a little while late Andy came back and he had a REAL live ad for us to work on. It was a small space newspaper ad for Kings Dominion theme park. The single minded idea? "If you buy a newspaper subscription, you get a free ticket to Kings Dominion." And it needed a headline.

By the last day of the internship, our small intern group nailed it. The winning headline was "Extra. Extra." The pun was perfect. And I honestly don't know if I came up with the headline or if another intern did. I think I convinced myself that it was my headline. Truth is, Andy Ellis probably wrote it himself in the bathroom and then spent a day trying to figure out how to convince us interns that we came up with it.

So in the end, it was Andy Ellis that gave me my first ad assignment. It was Andy who gave my first taste of that adrenaline that comes from creating an ad. It was Andy who got me hooked on the business.

But the truth is, it was Luke Sullivan who ultimately had the biggest impact on my career. Yes, I'm talking about the guy who just dumped a bunch of award annuals on a table and said, "Memorize these."

You see, I left high school and went to Washington & Lee University. A college that did not believe in advertising. Hell, mentioning advertising to my journalism professors was sacrilegious. So there were no courses on advertising. No text books. But I took those CA annuals to college. I got new ones along the way. And I studied them over and over.

I've read a lot of "instructional" type of books on creating ads and developing ideas over the years. (One of them written by Luke Sullivan.) And while some have been useful, I've never found any more helpful than simply looking at a ton of great work in an annual and absorbing the thinking.

But I also found these award annuals to be more than just educational. They became a set of standards for me. I started my career in a couple of agencies that really did mostly crappy work. And I had some people in those agencies telling me I was doing great work. To prove their point, they kept throwing more money at me. But those award show annuals told me the truth. They told me that my work was not good enough to be in them. While I might not have had a creative director early in my career to reject my work and push me to better ideas, those annuals kind of fulfilled that role.

In the end, my first ad was a small retail newspaper ad. But my first lesson from Luke Sullivan is the one that truly had the greatest impact on any success I've had in this business.

Janet Kestin
Co-founder of Swim

Janet Kestin was Co-Chief Creative Officer of Ogilvy Toronto before founding Swim, a creative leadership lab, with long-time partner Nancy Vonk in 2011.

They have won many top industry awards including Cannes Lions, One Show Pencils and Clios. They are the creative directors of Dove "Evolution", winner of two Grand Prix at Cannes, and "Diamond Shreddies, winner of a Grand Clio.

Janet has judged many of the world's top advertising awards shows including Cannes, Clios, One Show and D&AD.

Janet and Nancy's honors include being named to Creativity magazine's Top 50 creative people of '08, advertising Women of the Year at the WIN Awards in LA and the AWNY Awards in NY in '07, and induction into Canada's Marketing Hall of Legends in '11. Janet is a mentor and frequent lecturer at universities and ad schools including the renowned VCU Brandcenter.

Their widely read advice column, "Ask Jancy" on ad site ihaveanidea.org spawned critically acclaimed Adweek book, "Pick Me", in 2005. It has become a staple in advertising schools from Texas to Turkey. They are currently writing a business book for HarperCollins.

Janet Kestin, My Thoughts

To say that Janet Kestin is one of the nicest people you could ever meet is not an overstatement.

Canadians are nice anyway; but to give you an idea of just how nice Janet is, she won Gold at the Vancouver Olympics in the Nice Competition. Well, tied it, actually, with her creative partner, Nancy Vonk.

Once, when she didn't accept a formal, written offer for a very important position I was representing her for (as if there could be any other kind of positions that I would represent people for), she felt she had to do something nice to show her appreciation. So she sent me a big chocolate rabbit by way of consolation. Great. I gained no dollars, but did gain pounds (God, I hate myself for punning like that).

Janet first came to my attention after she and Nancy Vonk had created and launched that incredible DOVE campaign that swept the awards that year. But she was happy and staying put (the story of my life).

We spoke from time to time, then finally met for lunch in New York. She had her son, Devin, with her, and you could tell how proud she was of him. I thought my wife was proud of our son, but Janet was walking around with a big neon arrow pointing at Devin saying, "That's my son!"

And in what I do, it's unguarded, private moments like that that really give you insight into someone's heart.

I can't offer more than that. Incredible talent. Incredible nice. Isn't that enough?

My First Time (ish)
By Janet Kestin

PROLOGUE
Co-worker: So, what does your wife do for a living?
My husband: She writes ads.
Co-worker: You mean someone actually writes those things?

LOGUE (cute, I know)
Over the last few weeks, I've overturned drawers, ransacked closets, and conducted an archeological dig of my basement in an attempt to unearth the earliest evidence of my ad career. Eureka. A cracked, dusty, black portfolio peeks out from behind a pile of unused lumber, old stereo equipment, a couple of broken lamps, several tubs of childhood memorabilia and the box from a 20-year old Cuisinart. You can see how often I go down there.

The portfolio feels suspiciously light as I yank on the uncooperative zipper. A few sheets of yellowed paper slide out. Are they my first?

(Cue the wavy lines)

On that day, long ago, when I was riding the Montreal metro trying to decide what to do with my life, I didn't even know that advertising was a job. All I knew was that I was a pretty good writer and it was the only thing anyone might pay me for. I'd applied to newspapers (remember them?), magazines, television and radio stations. I was coming from an interview that didn't look all that promising, staring blankly at the mostly crap posters that run along the upper edge of subway cars. I thought ,"I could do better than that." Light bulb.

I went through the Yellow Pages. Called every ad agency in Montreal in alphabetical order to find out what I needed to do to apply for a job. I was all the way to "Y" before anyone agreed to talk to me. After showing me some of the work and delivering a mini-lecture on the business of advertising, the Creative Director of Y&R Montreal told me that if I wanted to work in advertising, I should "put together a book and stop dressing like a nun."

I didn't really know what a "book" was, but I'd seen a few nuns in my time and as far as I could tell none of them ever wore a red turtleneck dress. The whole experience was baffling. I holed up in my living room and wrote lines like "Butter makes a batter better". Ouch. My first crack at a portfolio had headlines so pun-filled that I'd fire myself in a second. Still, someone kinder than me gave me a shot.   Before I knew it, I was writing - you guessed it -credit card statement stuffers in prose so compelling that within weeks, I was promoted to writing inspirational matchbook covers for the Four Seasons hotel. "A night of perfect sleep is as rare as a perfect diamond, and more to be desired." You know the type of thing I mean. I toiled in my cubby, praying for a few fewer editor's red marks on my copy, my very own art director and and waiting for my big break.

I wish I could show you what it looked like when it came. It was a TV commercial for a dessert called Pudding in a Cloud- chocolate Jello pudding sitting on a cloud of Cool Whip. I was working with an art director for the first time. A very senior, very British, eccentric, artist-fashion photographer-film director-art director, obsessed with big blue skies and clouds. "Pudding in a Cloud" was a natural fit, I guess. My art director was many brilliant things, but he wasn't a teacher. I did what I was told: *read the brief, go to the meeting, try not to put your inexperienced foot in your mouth, keep it simple, keep it short, write it again, write it again, write it again, if there's nothing to say, sing it, find a voice that's memorable, try to say something intelligent, but not so intelligent that no one will understand it.* I wrote a simple set of lyrics about the floating dessert. The account guys wanted them changed. The clients wanted them changed again. The evolution of the storyboard. The endless tinkering. The art director-fashion photographer-film director. The editor cutting, splicing. The first music track, the second, the third.

If you work really hard, I'll bet you can imagine the heavenly blue sky, clouds drifting lazily across it, Pudding In A Cloud drifting equally lazily. I kid you not. That partnership didn't last. He wasn't a partnership sort of guy.

First-ish ad. Hopefully worst ad.

EPILOGUE
When I first noticed posters on the subway, I figured any idiot could come up with work like that. By the time I'd actually finished my first real ad, I figured

that no matter how bad it was, you deserved a Cannes Lion just for surviving the process.

At the end of my first year in my first real partnership, we were doing an inventory of what we'd accomplished. All we had to show for our blood, sweat and tears (mine), was four pieces of paper. One of them fell out of that old, cracked portfolio.

It was for Toro lawnmowers, which offered a technology that was new and different for its time.

The headline was "This is the only time you'll ever see a Toro broken down." It was an intelligent dissection of the lawnmower. It was no Cannes Lion, but it was no Pudding In A Cloud, either.

Dante Lombardi
Former ECD, Yahoo!

Dante Lombardi was born in Brooklyn, New York. Half Boston Irish, half N.Y. Italian. He grew up in Massachusetts. He went to Brandeis University and majored in painting. He has spent his career as an Art Director, Copywriter, and Creative Director, mostly at advertising agencies.

In New York, at Angotti, Thomas, Hedge and Korey, Kay and Partners. In N.Y. he learned his craft; Typography, design, photography, film, and music. He learned to fight for his ideas. He learned to love a crazy business. In Los Angeles, at BBDO. In L.A. he worked a lot, grew a little, and won lots of awards. He became a Copywriter. He learned to let his ideas speak for themselves.

In San Francisco, at Goodby, Silverstein and Partners, and McCann-Erickson. In S.F. he worked with the best, traveled the world, went digital and made work everyone everywhere, saw. He learned to help other people's ideas get made. He decided to leave a crazy business. Having worked on brands like Nike, Microsoft, hp, and Pepsi, in every medium, digital, traditional, big and small, he felt like he'd seen it all--except the client side. Now living in Berkeley with a wife and three sons, Silicon Valley beckoned. First TiVo, where he helped rebrand the company, and now Yahoo!, where he began in 2010 as VP/Executive Creative Director. While at Yahoo! he's built an internal creative department that handles virtually all of the brand's creative needs, including advertising, events, branding, environmental design and more.

Dante Lombardi, My Thoughts

First of all, anyone with a name like Dante Lombardi just has to be someone special.

A Felllini movie star, a philosopher/writer, a vintage chianti. Or, one of the people prescient enough to look at the nascent net, rub his chin and go: "Hmmm, I think this can be something and me thinks I'll tag along for the ride."

Well the last one is *our* Dante Lombardi.

As happens many times with recruiters, but, it seems, especially with me, Dante turned down an ECD position he was offered through me to become the ECD of YAHOO!   He had already been the ECD of TIVO and McCann/SF. But YAHOO! Yahoo!

Over his career so far, Dante has been at the forefront of creative technology. He's an expert at blending the net with the creative noggin. He works across so many different disciplines, you marvel how he keeps all the balls in the air and constantly moving in perfect synchronicity.

Which is what true integrated advertising is all about.

However, when you read Dante's story, you'll find it nauseating. Literally. You'll see.

So go get some Dramamine, buckle in and get ready for a rocky ride.

My First Time
By Dante Lombardi

Ship of Fools.

The ship heaved. I heaved. It was day three at sea sailing from Miami to Puerto Rico and I was bent over the railing on the starboard side of the Lido deck, retching. Mussels, brussel sprouts, prime rib, purple Peruvian mashed potatoes, smoked salmon, an ice cream sundae with butterscotch sauce and a pickled Michigan Bing cherry on top, white wine and red wine and three scotches and a shot of tequila; Over-drinking and over-eating are the two main attractions on a Caribbean cruise. Booting is the third.

I held weakly to the rail. It all came up, until only the dry, painful spasms remained. And still my head swam, my legs wobbled, I whined. I don't like ships or the sea, and I easily get seasick. I won't name the ship or the cruise line, but I was at sea, and sick, for the filming of a TV commercial. My first time.

Many more puked and slobbered and sobbed in their rooms, green but more privately miserable. The sea was rough, and had been for two days. The ship's stabilizers were turned on, and between their low gut-rumbling thrum, the gluttony and the stormy sea, seasickness had gripped many of the passengers and most of our production team. The director, the camera crew, the client, the creative director, the copywriter and me, all to one degree or another as sick as dogs.

It was a terrible idea for a TV commercial. A couple would be seen dancing, dining, gambling, snuggling. While they blissed-out on gourmet rack of lamb, ocean sun and rum drinks poolside, we'd cut to their suburban home, where an answering machine (this was 1995) recorded annoying messages from coworkers, friends and family. Cut back to the couple, unaware, unconcerned, and happy. It was dumb. Most commercials are, but this was an especially lame idea. I didn't know any better and I didn't care. I was going on a shoot on a cruise.

The first day at sea had seemed a dream. There is food everywhere on a cruise ship, so I ate. The booze onboard would be covered by an expense account, (this was 1995) so I drank. We sat in the sun and planned the shoot and partied all night. This was why I had gone into advertising, to work with creative, interesting people on exciting projects in exotic places. It seemed lucrative, glamorous, and not terribly demanding.

Day two and filming commenced and everything went wrong. The Director was a control freak, but more Hitler than Kubrick. The passengers, sunburned and mostly homely, gawked and got in the shots, but on Captain's orders weren't to be inconvenienced in any way. The sea became rough, which showed in the pool scene, our actor struggling to swim as the pool's contents sloshed dramatically. The sea whipped up and it began to thunder and rain, cancelling the exterior shots. The sea began to roll, and we gobbled Dramamine, but to little effect.

The actors, sweating and beleaguered by dehydration and nausea, stumbled as they danced, grimaced as they feigned interest in Alaskan King Crab legs, and made no apparent attempt whatsoever to act as though they were having a good time.

Finally, the sea and the storm took over, and we all retreated to our cabins or the bar; I wandered alone through the ship, woozy, and prayed for death. Day three was more of the same. Dizziness, exhaustion, malaise; The misery seemed permanent now, something to function under in spite of, a new way of being. Seasickness is more than physical; it becomes a form of deep existential madness. Will it ever go away? Can misery be any deeper, or more complete? We caught it all on film. We had captured the reality, but it would make a poor case for our clients.

Day four and the storm broke, the sea quieted, and we started to return to normal, if a little traumatized. But it was too late. The shoot was over. We had what we had and we knew it was bad. We told each other we would find greatness from the footage, that despite the problems, it was "in there". It was just a thing to say, not at all believable.

Solid land appeared in the distance at midday that day, and I rejoiced. The team disembarked in Puerto Rico, and we all flew home to edit the film.

The spot never aired. But I had gone on a shoot on a cruise.

Dom Maiolo
Executive Creative Director, Leo Burnett/Chicago

(Dom is the one on the right)

Dom has been working for the Leo Burnett Company since 1982. He started as a Copywriter and made his way to ECD. In that time he has worked on many brands: Miller Lite, Pillsbury, Sony, Kellogg's, General Motors, PM, P&G, McDonald's, WalMart and most notably Nintendo. He has worked on Nintendo since 1994. He was on the team that launched Pokemon in the US in 1998. He has also launched Nintendo DS, Nintendo DSi and the Nintendo Wii. Awards included Cannes, Clio, Addy, One Show, and a Grand Effie for Nintendo Wii. He lives in Long Grove, IL with his wife Jil, son Jack and daughter Lila.

Dom Maiolo, My Thoughts

Dom calls me his "consigliere". I'm honored. But he may be setting me up to get whacked. You never can tell with Dom. Which is what makes him so interesting.

He's like an Italian leprechaun.

When you think he'll zig, he zags.

When he laughs he breaks the known laws of physics: he inhales, exhales and grunts all at the same time. If you didn't know it was a laugh, you'd think he was having a heart attack or Mt. Vesuvius was erupting.

Dom and I have been friends for close to twenty years and we should both get an award. Or a citation for a moving violation.

Dom loves what he does, loves Nintendo, *lives* Nintendo and has been at Burnett so long he has his own apple tree.

He falls into the category of he'll give you the shirt off his back (which isn't too appetizing) if you work hard and do great work. But if you don't work hard, you don't want to know the alternative.

Yet in all the years I've known him, I've never heard one bad word said about him. Several, yes, but never just one.

Obviously, I'm having fun writing about Dom, because that's Dom.

Just wait till you read his story.

You'll hear him inhaling/exhaling/grunting all the way through.

My First Time
By Dom Maiolo

This first time is coming to you from the 1980s. Leo Burnett in the 1980s to be exact. Ho Ho Ho Green Giant. Poppin' Fresh Pillsbury Doughboy Marlboro Man 1980s. A different time really. The day-to-day back then was so different than it is now. We were more social back then. There were more lunches. More drunken incidents. Or maybe it was just because I was in my 20's and behaved differently, but I swear to God we work harder now. This was life before the holding company. The bench was so deep at Burnett back then guys went years without ever selling anything. Ted Bell was there. John Eding was there. Jim Ferguson was there. And just being around these guys did two things to you.

1. Scared the hell out of you.
2. Made you better.

I was working on Oldsmobile .

I went from writing scripts for auto show girls to working on the mainline stuff that included TV and print. I was 25 yrs old. My cubicle was on the 7th floor of the Prudential Building. There were over 300 creatives on that floor in those days. It was the biggest creative department housed in one space in the days before Photoshop, InDesign and QuickTime. Writers typed on royals or IBM selectrics and Art Directors did their own boards most of them in magic marker, but some in oils or water colors. And they all smoked. Everybody smoked.

My art director partner on this job was an older guy. He reminded me of Keith Richards. Always smoking. Always laughing. Always saying something you couldn't quite understand. He used to end most of his sentences with "you know what I'm saying?", because half of the time you never did. He had a boozy unconscious coolness about him that made you feel like you were hanging out with a guy who saw the world differently. He did. He saw it as light and shapes. He saw it as color.

We were shooting a Cutlass Supreme spot in White Sands, NM. Back then the

Oldsmobile spots were a formula, so even a guy like me had a chance at selling one. The formula was simple :

Car. Babe. Car. Babe. Fluttercut to the logo. Car. Babe. Done.

The idea was that the Cutlass was so smooth it made every ride a downhill run. Like skiing. Thus the white sands. We were going shoot the Cutlass swooshing around the White Sands doing big S turns. Easy.

Back then flying first class was policy. A mandate. We were Leo Burnett and we flew first class on United Airlines; another Burnett client.

You didn't have corporate credit cards back then, either. Instead, they gave you a big wad of travelers' checks. For my week in White Sands they gave me $3000. I had never seen that much money. To me it was 6 months rent. I carried the American Express travelers' check wallet in my front pocket scared someone was going to hit me over the head and take it.

We flew to El Paso, Texas . Drove to White Sands. I met the director Werner Hlinka . He was a car shooter. He also shot a movie called "Cheerleaders Beach Party" back in the 70s. Everyone on set spoke a different language they spoke "production".

I learned new phrases like "golden hour" - it was what we waited for to shoot the beauty shots of the Cutlass. "Craft Service" - it was this amazing table that held amazing snacks you could eat all day. "Honey Wagon" - it was the trailer you visited after too much time at the craft service table eating snacks and drinking espresso .

I was having the time of my life. I kept trying to keep up with these guys drink for drink at the bar at night. Huge mistake. My creative director was a big guy. Large man. All-American defensive tackle large man. He was twice my size and what you would call a "crazy motherfucker". At Burnett he was famous for doing things like this: after a boozy lunch on the walk back from the restaurant, he picked up his secretary and held her by the ankles over the Michigan Avenue Bridge. Later that same year he took my then-girlfriend and me to dinner. After a couple of martinis he said to the two of us. "Hey why don't you two come and spend the weekend up at my house. My wife and I wouldn't mind watching you fuck." Ha ha ha. He was nuts. We never made it to his house.

Drinking with a guy like him was suicide, but I kept at it with more than the usual dedication. I was so hung-over on the second day of the shoot I left my $3000 in travelers' checks in the production motor home and forgot about them until two days later. Thank God they were all there.

Always looking for some kind of thrill my creative director felt the whole spot needed something and wanted to see some more action. Something visual. Something surprising. While we were all off smoking he got the idea that we should jump the car. Build a ramp and have the car fly through the air. He told the producer.

The producer told the production company. The production company sent the car tech guy over who told us it was risky. Oldsmobile only sent down the one car. If we damaged the car jumping it the shoot would be over. They didn't build those cars to handle things like jumps. That's what the car tech guy told us.

My creative director didn't want to jeopardize the shoot but wanted to jump the car. Werner Hlinka suggested we make it our last shot. So that's what we did. After two days of shooting the Cutlass doing S turns on the White Sands we built a ramp, got a couple of cameras in place and talked to the precision driver about doing the jump.

She had never jumped a car before and was glad we were doing the shot last . Golden Hour of the second day came. We were ready to go. The precision driver aimed the Cutlass at the ramp. The cameras rolled. Her approach was a bit off. She didn't hit the ramp dead center. She hit it too far inside.

The Cutlass flew through the air. My creative director was hooting and hollering, but when the Cutlass landed it hit wrong. And it bounced. Hard! So hard, a strut blew through the top of the drivers' side quarter panel, blowing the tire as it met the sheet metal and the Cutlass swerved out of control. The precision driver bounced off of the steering wheel. She was almost knocked out cold. And the Cutlass plugged itself into one of the white pristine sand dunes. Crash landing.

I didn't know what to think but my CD was going mental over the fact that we jumped the Cutlass and got it on film. And that was my first time. I flew first class. Misplaced $3000. Crashed a car into a sand dune. And learned you can fix everything in post.

Kevin McKeon
Executive Creative Director, StrawberryFrog/NY

A 30-year veteran of advertising, Kevin McKeon rebounded from his first shameful advertising experience, and has gone on to work at the best creative agencies in New York, including BBH, BBDO, Ammirati and Puris, and Scali, McCabe, and Sloves. His work on brands like Levi's, Axe, Mercedes-Benz, Schweppes, Rolling Stone, Heineken, Jim Beam, Virgin Atlantic Airways and Johnny Walker has been recognized by every major advertising award show. He's served on the boards of The One Club and The Art Directors Club, has taught at New York's School of Visual Arts, and is, as of this writing, Chief Creative Officer of Strawberryfrog/New York, an agency known for daring, unconventional creative thinking, across both traditional and emerging media.

Kevin McKeon, My Thoughts

Hopefully, you've read Kevin's bio. It reads more like a testimonial. All those top agencies and awards and accomplishments.

However, to me, Kevin is Mr. Not Interested. That's what I'd get from him every time I called with another incredible opportunity. However, since he was already *in* an incredible opportunity, it was kind of like bringing coals to Newcastle.

In any event, when one (or as many as you like) looks at Kevin's work over the years, you see humor, daring, a creative director who's not afraid to take chances and who has the ability to have his clients take them, as well. And all with a plentiful payoff.

Kevin's work ranges from a bizarre-athoned Willem Defoe for Jim Beam to Match.com. From Mentos to the Emirates. Talk about range. Or dementia precox.

Though I don't know Kevin very well, he gave me permission to make up a story about him; so I will.

Kevin and I happened to be having a drink at one of Manhattan's tonier watering holes when one of the most beautiful women (other than my wife) walked in and fell to the ground in a dead faint.

Kevin was immediately upon her (that doesn't sound right), giving her mouth-to-mouth and CPR, mouth-to-mouth and CPR. Probably the only time he wouldn't have been arrested for fondling.

Anyway, the woman finally awoke, thanked Kevin for saving her life, and, as it turned out, she was the sister of the CEO of one of the biggest accounts in the world, and she was there to meet her brother for lunch.

When her brother found out what Kevin had done, he gave him the account right then and there and Kevin lived happily ever after.

And I have a bridge to sell you in Brooklyn, too.

My First Time
By Kevin McKeon

Looking back, I was kind of an asshole. I didn't see it then, but I imagine that's not unusual. I've seen other young creatives who are also assholes, and I'm sure they don't think of themselves that way.

I was 21 at the time, having spent a couple of years at School of Visual Arts, and I thought I knew everything there was to know about advertising. Certainly more than the owner of the small advertising agency along Route 18 in New Jersey, where I managed to land my first job as a copywriter, that first summer out of school. I can't even remember how I got the job, or heard about the agency in the first place, but I do remember that it was a tiny place, maybe half a dozen people, and it serviced mostly a local retail clientele - carpet stores, local bakeries, local bank, that sort of thing. Newspaper print ads, maybe a little local radio - that was pretty much it. The owner did most of the illustrations for the ads himself. And he kept a copy of The One Show Annual on the reception table, open to a print campaign that was a finalist a few years back. That was his claim to fame. I was the sole copywriter, sharing a small room in the back with the office supplies and a coffee pot. I earned a rookie's salary and worked by myself, 50 miles and a world away from the glamorous New York advertising career I had envisioned for myself.

And you know what? I should have felt lucky to have the job. Because at that point in my career, I had a lot more to learn that I had to offer. Even when it came to this tiny New Jersey advertising agency. I just didn't realize it at the time.

I remember one moment specifically, the turning point for me. My boss, the owner of the agency, the guy who chased down the business, who wrote most of the ads and illustrated most of the art, the one-man-band who did pretty much everything that needed to get done, had taken a couple of my print comps to a client, along with what I thought was some pretty clever copy. When he returned, he put the ads on my desk, marked up with copy changes, and asked me to make the appropriate revisions.

My response? "The next time you present my work to a client, I'd appreciate it if you'd at least consult me before you agree to make any changes."

I know, I know. Asshole.

Now, as someone who's been writing advertising copy for a long time, I could sit here and take a credible stab at rationalizing my response. Creative integrity. Perfectionist. Uncompromising. A guy who, even then, knew the meaning of "death by 1,000 cuts." But I know the truth.

When did I first know? 30 seconds after the fact, when he fired me. Suddenly I wasn't a guy working at a small New Jersey ad agency, sharing a room with FedEx boxes and a coffee pot; I was a guy *fired* from a small New Jersey ad agency, no longer sharing a room with Fed Ex boxes and a coffee pot. Nice work, hotshot New York ad school guy. And oh, by the way, those ads that I was so indignant about? They sucked.

I deserved what I got.

The good news? That was the moment I peaked as an asshole. I like to think I learned my lesson, right there, along Route 18 in New Jersey, and (hopefully) have since mended my asshole ways.

You might be asking, why does it even matter? We can all name a few legendary assholes - screaming lunatics, soul crushing bullies, relentless micro-managers - who also happen to be legendary, even iconic, asshole geniuses. Isn't that the only thing that truly matters, doing great work, even if a few people get offended along the way?

Yes. Well... maybe. Maybe if you're the next Steve Jobs, or Mark Zuckerberg, or Anna Wintour, or John McEnroe. But chances are, you're not. Chances are, you're just like me - one of the 99 9/10% of the rest of the world, out there trying to distinguish yourself from a very competitive, very talented, and very hungry pack. Why risk it?

When I interview young advertising creatives, that's one thing I'm always wary of: the asshole factor. I'll take a super-hungry but unproven young creative, someone who's eager to learn and willing to do anything for the privilege, before I'll hire someone with an impressive body of work, but whose first questions are, "What will I be working on?," and "How many people will I have to report to?" Because already I'm thinking, well... you know.

And here's some more solid advice for all you would-be assholes out there. It's not just about getting your first job. When it comes time to lay someone off, all things being relatively equal, it's usually the asshole who gets tapped on the shoulder. When a client asks someone off his business, it's usually because he thinks that person is, well... kind of an asshole - even if he doesn't say it out loud. And when an asshole falls, no one reaches out to pick him back up.

You're on your own, asshole.

Why be the guy everybody WANTS to see fail? Advertising (and any business, really) is a small - and very competitive - world. And there are a lot of good creatives out there competing for the same jobs you want. Don't handicap yourself. It's often the little things that separate the truly successful from the struggling middle of the pack.

Work hard. Stay curious. Constantly challenge yourself. Don't ever get too comfortable.

And for god's sake, don't shoot yourself in the foot. Don't be an asshole.

Darren Moran
Former ECD, draftfcb, New York

Darren Moran is a 22-year veteran writer and Creative Director who has created some of the most innovative brand experiences in TV, digital and print, across every client category imaginable. From 2010 to 2012, as the Chief Creative Officer of Draftfcb New York, Moran won integrated pitches for Gevalia Coffee, the US Freeskiing team and The Jamaica Tourist Board, as well as snaring Digital AOR duties for Barclaycard and Eucerin. Under his leadership, the agency's improved creative work for Oreo and Gerber were noted repeatedly in the trades and mainstream press. While at DFCB, Moran also helped create new campaigns for The Office of National Drug Control Policy, Fisher-Price, Nivea and the U.S. Census.

Prior to Draftfcb, Moran was a Global CD at Young & Rubicam, where he created award-winning campaigns for LG, Xerox, Chevron, Bacardi, Burger King, Cellular South, AT&T, MTV and many others. He was a member of the Y&R Global Creative Board and won the NY office's first One Show pencils in 20 years, and the Y&R network's first (and second) Integrated awards. His Cannes Lions for LG also contributed to Y&R NY becoming the second most awarded agency in the world in 2010. While at Y&R, Moran led the successful pitches for the LG, Cellular South, Chevron, Office Depot and Goldman Sachs accounts. He started his career at BBDO, where he worked on GE, Visa, Hyatt, Frito-Lay and Pizza Hut, helping the shop win Agency of the Year from both AdWeek and AdAge. Moran has won every major industry award, has judged several shows and is a member of the CRC of The Partnership at drugfree.org.

Darren Moran, My Thoughts

Darren is one of those people you meet and immediately like. The kind of person you want to sit and have a drink with, even if your great-grandmother was Carrie Nation.

In contravention to my telling him that he's a really nice guy, Darren warned me that he's not so easy on people he perceives as not doing what they should be doing. I understand that, but he's never run around shouting like the Red Queen, "Off with his head! Off with his head!" A finger will do.

In fact, and I never told him this, one of his people told me that everything Darren touches, he makes better. Think of that. And the guy said it without payment.

On a personal level, he's quick to laugh (and it's a big, boisterous, broiling Irish laugh), quick to commiserate, and on a professional level, he's quick to understand a client's needs and how to respond best to those needs. And while I've never seen him in action, I've been told he puts on such a show that Broadway is beckoning. But I don't think Hugh Jackman has anything to worry about.

Darren would be first to say "Pshaw!" about this, but then again, he would have to be the first because how many people do you know who go around saying "Pshaw!"?

My First Time
By Darren Moran

When he was born, he measured five feet eight inches long. Three male nurses were called in just to weigh him, as he tipped the scales at 172 pounds 9 ounces. Not long after the delivery, the doctors conferred in serious tones about his five o'clock shadow. Odd if for no other reason than it was ten o'clock in the morning. Witnesses swear he cut his own umbilical cord then handed the scissors back to the doctor, handle-side out.

Yes, you guessed it. That baby was me. Bigger, older-looking, and more "responsible" than everyone else my age, which has been the case pretty much my whole life. And it's how I ended up on my first shoot.

I was barely out of college and working at a huge, famous Madison Avenue shop when I found myself part of a team that wrote an "anthem"-type commercial with lots of locations around the country. I got picked to go to Hawaii to shoot a couple of the scenes, unsupervised. Now, I cannot stress enough how little I knew of the process after a script got bought, but no one seemed to realize that. My bosses shouldn't be blamed for this failure of judgment any more than the head of my college radio station could be blamed for handing me my own morning show despite having never interned, the result of which was a very uncomfortable and apparently illegal 15 minutes of "dead air" on my first day. You see, by this point I was well over nine feet tall and looked to be in my early 40s and, possibly, a wildebeest. No one questioned whether or not I was ready.

But as was my way, I kept my mouth shut, packed a valise full of Hawaiian shirts (so I'd really fit in!), and took my very first trip in First Class, a ticket that cost more than my annual salary. I stayed in a hotel that I knew was fancy because it had a second floor and a pool *in* the ground instead of on it. Despite my greenness, I quickly learned what a mini bar was when I ate a jar of what I thought were free macadamia nuts sitting on my nightstand. My stomach knotted up when I saw I was charged $20 (roughly 12,000 in today's dollars), a sum I was sure I would be fired over. When it came time to rent a car as an under-aged renter, again, no questions asked except "Would you like two cars, sir, one for each foot?" To make up for the Macadamia Incident I took the cheapest vehicle they had, a Bulgarian hatchback or equivalent. Later, I was shocked by the Volvos and BMW's in which everyone else from the agency showed up. I'm not kidding. The valet actually wrote "basura" (Spanish for "garbage.") on my claim ticket. I started parking on the street just to avoid his very hurtful taunts.

So here I was in beautiful Hawaii, learning a ton about advertising before we had shot even a foot of film. Or so I thought. Once we got down to the business of the actual shoot, I started to realize how little I really knew. There must have been 30 people gathered for the first agency/production company meeting prior to the pre-pro the next day. Everyone seemed important, carrying lots of forms and clipboards and Polaroids of things paper clipped to other things. They looked like they had been doing this since cigarette commercials featured doctors and astronauts, which, of course, many of them had. The Cinematographer just won an Oscar. The director had an expensive-looking viewfinder on a gold chain around his neck and a wall full of awards that smelled of fresh polish. All I carried were two Bic pens and cocktail napkins from the hotel bar because I had forgotten my notebook. I was in shorts and a Hawaiian shirt. Everyone else was wearing jeans and non-ridiculous shirts. Some even had slacks. Actual grown-up slacks. Only one person in the whole joint was wearing a trucker hat that read "I Got Lei'd in Hawaii." I think you know who that was. I prayed I was coming off as someone with the breezy, confident, devil-may-care attitude made possible only by a trunkful of Lions or a trust fund. But in reality I don't think anyone gave a shit what I looked like.

Which is Lesson #1 in this business: it doesn't matter where you came from, only what you're doing right now. Be great in the moment.

The shots we needed were pretty simple, save for one in which some dolphins had to leap on cue. I was pretty sure this wasn't my job so I stayed out of that discussion, other than to make a mental note that I was going to "try some wild lines" with the dolphins as my boss was always telling me to make sure I got a lot of wild lines so we had options in the edit. I don't know why people say dolphins are so smart; they're terrible at improv, in my experience.

Luckily most of the other questions that came up were aimed at the director, on account of the viewfinder and the air of respectability a viewfinder automatically confers. I surmised that I, too, would need an accouterment if I were going to get far in this business, and made a mental note to look into eye patches and capes when I got back to the mainland.

But about halfway through the meeting a decision had to be made, and apparently I was the only one who could make it. I needed to pick which bathing suit a little boy in the scene would wear. It wasn't a difficult decision but, again, *having never done this before,* I wasn't expecting to be making decisions of any kind, let alone this kind. I started to choke.

There were two choices which, to my eye came down to: Red. Or, yellow. A hush fell over the entire group as they awaited my Solomonic decision. Suggesting we split the difference and get an orange one didn't even occur to me in that moment. I could feel my face turning flush with embarrassment and my palms getting sweaty. I did that cock your head left, then right, thing to appear I was evaluating the choices from different angles, if only to buy some time to figure out what the right answer was. I rubbed my chin, held each pair of trunks up in the light like a fine Bordeaux. I came dangerously close to swirling the bathing suits to see how they "opened up." Thank God I didn't sniff them; you live with a move like that the rest of your career.

Mr. Academy Award started to wander off. I could sense I was losing the group, especially the director, which you never, ever want to do. If the director loses confidence in you, you can kiss that spot goodbye.

And it was in this instance that I realized Lesson #2: There is no right or wrong decision. There is only *your* decision. It's your spot. You created it, you own it, for good or bad.

"Yellow," I said with the most confidence a guy in a flowered shirt can legitimately pull off. And, remembering the location Polaroids, added, "It will pop better against the blue waterslide." It might have only been me that felt a collective sign of relief in the room as we moved on to other things, and more decisions. But, at least for a moment, I had moved the ball a yard forward and it felt good. Whatever confidence anyone had in me suddenly didn't feel so misplaced. And I finally got it: Foreign cars and fancy nuts and the chance to command humans in a life-sized game of chess-to-the-death are all relatively meaningless. *This* is why we're in this business.

Which brings me to Lesson #3: live in the deep end of the pool. If no one accidentally pushes you in because you're big and look like you know what you're doing, jump in yourself. It's the only way to learn. You'll make mistakes and be better for it. If the job ever starts to feel easy, or you're not regularly scared shitless, then you've wandered into the shallow end. Get to the other end immediately and start swallowing some water.

Finally, if you remember only one thing, please remember this: a hat that says "I Got Lei'd in Hawaii" makes a terrible souvenir for your girlfriend's mother.

Trust me.

John O'Keeffe
WPP Worldwide Creative Director

I started my career at Saatchi, moving with my then partner Russell Ramsey (now ECD JWT London) to an up and coming outfit called BBH in 1990. I stayed there for eighteen years, ultimately becoming ECD in 2000. During the next few years the agency doubled in size and garnered fourteen agency of the year titles from various sources, including a unique hat-trick from industry bible, Campaign Magazine. I hasten to add that, as with all such achievements, it was very much a joint effort. More importantly, it was there I met my future wife Jane, who has since account handled my life with great skill, and with whom I have two wonderful children Charlotte and James, both of whom I am training to become avid Arsenal fans, like their dear old dad!

John O'Keeffe, My Thoughts

As is often the case with people I interact with, but who dwell in far-off climes, John and I hadn't met. We had conversed over the years and I always found him to be courteous, considerate, and a possessor of a great sense of incisive humor.

But I was in London for business recently, and, of course, it was a priority to meet John.

Now I had, on the day before, walked the floors of the House of Commons and the House of Lords, and being a great student of British history, with each step I felt the presence of Churchill, Disraeli, Lloyd George, Gladstone, you get the idea.

Then, upon meeting John the very next morning, I was back in Parliament. Though he was casually dressed and greeted me warmly and convivially, I felt as if I was meeting an important MP (should I curtsy?)

I thought this couldn't just be a VIP Global CD for WPP. No, this eminence relaxing in his executive chair was about to put forth a bill which would change the fortunes of the entire British Empire.

I then remembered there was no British Empire any longer; but no matter how much our conversation remained in the sphere of the empire of advertising, after John would expound so intelligently on one point or another, I had to stop myself from shouting: "Hear, hear! Hear, hear!"

So my question now is, if John should run for Parliament, how can an American vote for him?

My First Time
By John O'Keeffe

Pre-Story:
In a spare 45mins between launching News International's latest newspaper knocked this out. I'm sure you have a lot of *"it was perfect"* type stuff. So here's an antidote. My first time sadly wasn't Citizen Kane, but I quite liked it (though I haven't seen it in twenty years).

The Story
I always worry that, if the police were to suddenly show up and ask -- *"where were you on the evening of the nineteenth?"* -- I'd probably be staring at the wrong end of a stretch at Her Majesty's pleasure. Because I suspect my answer would be a mumbled, *"dunno, can't remember."* I might ask: *"what was on the TV that night? I was probably sitting in front of it."* Whereupon, with my arm bent up behind my back, I'd be thrown into the meat wagon to the echo of *"That's what they all say!"*

It's in that spirit of general amnesia that I approach the question of "My first time."

And I am transported back to 1985 (or was it '86? — there, I told you the memory was going.) and the Black and Decker power tools account held by Saatchi & Saatchi. James Lowther, still a Saatchi stalwart, had given me my first job in advertising, and a 30 second spot for Black and Decker's jig-saw was my first TV job.

At this stage I want to issue a warning: I'm afraid I've never been of an overly florid disposition re advertising. It's a job, a great job, but a job nonetheless. You do the best you can in the circumstances, and sometimes they give you an award, which is nice. But ultimately we're in the sales business. So, dear reader, if you're hoping for a tale of passionate argument with an overbearing director, or a death or glory defence of my art, then I'm sure other chapters will fulfill your every desire. And if they don't, you can always rent "The Agony & The Ecstasy" - I find it's much easier to become overwrought about The Sistine Chapel than power tools.

Back then we all worked hard, did our jobs and, pretty well every night, repaired to The Carpenter's Arms round the corner for a swift half. Saatchis, mid-80s, for a young copywriter, was blood sweat and beers.

Back to the commercial. At the time there was a British ice skating duo called Torvill and Dean who, to the accompaniment of Ravel's Bolero, had won something very big somewhere - probably the Winter Olympics -- and the whole country was desperately proud of them. I can't recall getting particularly worked up about it, but I did happen to notice two things that linked these ice-borne Olympians to power tools: specifically the jig-saw.

The first thing related to the product's great claim to fame: it could cut through sheet metal. And sheet metal, with the right lighting, could be made to look like ice. The second thing was that, if you inverted the brand name, it had the same syllable rhythm as Torvill and Dean. Thus the "Decker and Black" ice skating commercial, complete with Ravel's Bolero, and voiced by the bloke who always did the commentary on ice skating, was born. Very nice, too.

Not exactly a legend. More a sort of "never-out-of-work character actor who, nonetheless, will always stand some way behind Brad Pitt at the premier".

Can't remember who the director was, but he did a nice enough job with minimal fuss, and we both moved on to the next project, having parted on good terms. Take note Rex Harrison and Charlton Heston, and sundry ad luvvies too tedious to mention!

I believe D.I.Y stores ran out of Black and Decker jig-saws the weekend the ad broke, and the client was very happy although, in the famed industry jargon, it didn't trouble any juries.

Better things followed over the years (and, if I'm honest, some worse).

It was however the start of a career, and I've somehow managed to cling on to a job in the creative department ever since.

167

Rob Rasmussen
Chief Creative Officer, U.S., Tribal DDB

Robert Rasmussen, Tribal DDB's Chief Creative Officer Tribal DDB U.S, has had a career that has been hard to categorize. He began as a designer, became an art director, working in the most creative traditional and digital agencies. On his way to creative director, he has won nearly every top creative and effectiveness awards in the industry. Rasmussen's notable contributions to the evolution of digital creative excellence include "Beta-7" for Sega, created while at Weiden + Kennedy, was named in the Book of Tens:Best Non-TV Campaigns of the Decade recently by Advertising Age. Prior to joining Tribal DDB, Rasmussen was the Executive Creative Director of Innovation at BBH New York, over-seeing the launch of Ally Bank and the global relaunch of the Sprite brand. Before that he served as Executive Creative Director at R/GA overseeing all of its Nike business which included the much lauded Nike Plus, the creation of the Nike.com platform and everything else form basketball to e-commerce.

Previously, as creative director at JWT, New York, Robert led the creative pitch for the Jetblue business there and oversaw the account until 2007. During this time he created and oversaw the "Sincerely, JetBlue" work which included the JetBlue Storybooth that gathered the content that was the basis for over 12 television commercials, 4 viral videos and in-flight content. Robert is an active member of the Board of Directors of the New York Art Directors Club and the CRC Ad Council. He has sat on juries for One Show, the Clios, Cannes, the International Andy Awards, the New York Festivals and the London International Awards.

Rob Rasmussen, My Thoughts

Rob Rasmussen, as you've seen from his bio, has been ECD so often his wife took to embroidering the letters on his shirts. Then he went and spoiled it by becoming North American CCO of Tribal DDB.

More embroidering.

Rob is the kind of person who invites his people to art gallery openings because it would be fun for them. And for him to see them having fun.

He does seminars for the 4As to ECDs of smaller shops in smaller markets, just to give them insights into how larger shops are operating, solving problems and clueing the ECDs in to new digital and integrated techniques.

He has a pet beta on his desk named Buddy. After his brother.

He has one of the biggest smiles and impish grins that some clients have tried to brand and bottle.

And under his guidance, Tribal DDB/NY invented an interactive advertising tool that can be used by any client, for any product, to any market, at any time. And while this was mere whimsy, you'd be surprised how well it works.

Rob also fosters such an atmosphere of creative camaraderie that he once hired a Hatfield and a McCoy and they became a team.

Has anyone in advertising won a Nobel Peace Prize?

My First Time
By Rob Rasmussen

I guess you could say, the first job I took at Wieden + Kennedy was a demotion. They offered me a position as a designer/ production artist and I was then a Junior Art Director. But one glimpse of a chance to work at the creative mecca of Ad land, the place that coined "Just Do It" and so much more, it took me about 8 minutes to quit my job and start packing to move north.

I had scored the interview through knowing a studio manager who was tasked to build a world-class studio. Wieden had just won Microsoft and needed to staff up. The portfolio I showed them was all spec. A collection of sketches and ideas I thought at the time should have been printed in the front of the One Show annuals. In retrospect, I suppose they'd have been better suited for the back of the recycling bin.

Most of the creatives walking the halls in those days have since gone on to run or be part of the best creative agencies in existence. Some of the names on the doors were Riswold, Barrett, Jay, Curtis, Keopke and McBride just to name drop a few. Back then, no one around the office read ADWEEK or even cared what other agencies where doing, their focus was on creation. A long filing cabinet outside reception was filled with Pencils, Lions and other pretty pieces of precious Ad metal, all sitting in a pile collecting dust.

That was a pressure that leaned heavily on my shoulders when I was promoted to Art Director, on the infamous Nike account. I remember the first project my partner Brian Ford and I sold in like it was yesterday. It was a holiday print ad for Niketown. Our ad showed Nike athletes visiting Santa with dreams of glorious products dancing through their heads. Pete Sampras was sitting in Santa's lap, looking up with glazed eyes as he told him of his holiday desires. Lisa Leslie was next in line impatiently waiting as other various athletes followed behind. The project itself was small, but to us, it meant everything.

One of Wieden's great abilities as an agency was to craft ideas into works of art. Marni in art buying had us hooked up with an up and coming photographer, Chris Buck, who on shoot day, seamlessly turned a West LA studio in into a winter wonderland. The Santa he had cast was better than the one I'd dreamt about as a kid. Real beard, real rosy cheeks and really jolly. When he smiled, you did too. Lisa Leslie arrived early. All seemed to be coming together perfectly. (I had clearly forgotten to knock on wood.)

Pete was running late and our defensive lineman from the Raiders had conflicting brand contracts. Sure he wore Nike shoes, but he was already sponsored with Oakley for sunglasses and another company for watches. Niketown sold both of those. It wasn't going to work. Our only choice was to cast a 'look-alike.' One with a square jaw ho could fill out a XXL jersey and stand at 6'0. Not an easy task with less than an hour to spare.

An hour goes by, no Faux-Oakland Raider, still no Pete and we then noticed the source of Santa's rosy cheeks was from consuming too much egg nog. That's when I noticed our Photographer, Chris Buck eying me up. I looked over at our client who was doing the same. I then notice the stylist and the prop girl staring at me. Finally, Chris broke the stare and said: "You know, you look just like a pro footballer..." No way. But after a couple drinks with Kris Kringle, I obliged.

Pete Sampras was an idol of mine. I had admired him as a professional athlete and knew he was destined to go down as one of the best tennis players in history. I had practiced my introduction to him many times in my head. I had thought about shooting the breeze a bit, then take him through the concept, coaching him on how to look off camera, allowing his acting side to show. But as time wore on without him there, I had to be transformed into the Oakland Football player, complete with padded pants, lace up cleats shoulder pads. The make up girl added the black smudges under my eyes. This was not how I imagined meeting Pete.

With less than an hour studio time left, Pete flies in like a hurricane. We are introduced and I start to explain the creative idea but he interrupts. "Why are we fucking listening to Christmas music?" He disappears out the door and returns moments later with a Pearl Jam CD which he then throws on stereo and cranks it from 4 decibels to 10. He then takes a seat in Santa's lap and is ready to go. I remind Chris to stress the child like gaze versus looking into camera. He nods and whispers to Pete who nods too.

Flash. Flash. Flash. Over a hundred shots have popped off and Pete is still staring directly into camera. Standing in the pads, sweating my black grease paint off, I am slowly dying and so is my print ad. Finally, I see a good time to run behind the camera and talk to Chris. My cleats click- clack across the floor as I once again tell Chris to stress Pete not looking into camera.

Pete sees me talking to Chris and yells "What the fuck?! "Seriously, what the fuck is up with the football player? This is my fucking ad. I'm the Hall of Famer." Pete was then shot in the neck with a tranquilizer.

No, actually he was talked down by the client, photographer and his agent. Shattered were my dreams of attending his New Year's party that year, but such is life.

After that last direction, he nailed it. A finger raised ever so delicately to his chin while he looked dreamingly up into the air as Santa cradled his six foot plus frame. Pete showed he is indeed a real Pro. We finally wrapped. And I finally exhaled.

I thought I was going to die that day. It would have been a short life in advertising for me. But somehow we all survived. Proof that no matter how well planned a shoot is, Murphy's Law is always there to punch your plan in the face. But that's part of experiencing life and being able to move forward with a notch on your belt. Which then becomes another great story to tell in the wild and zany world of advertising.

Marcus Rebeschini
Chief Creative Officer, Y&R Asia

In 2006, *Campaign Brief Asia* named him Advertising Person of the Year for consistent creative excellence over a two-year period, and ranked him as the number one creative in Asia Pacific. His work has won hundreds of industry accolades and a host of best of shows, and his campaigns have been ranked numerous times in the top 20 most awarded campaigns in the world by the *Gunn Report*.

Marcus returned to Asia in 2008, fresh from a successful stint with TBWA/Chiat/Day in New York with another Gold Lion from Cannes to his credit, and back to the scene of some of his greatest successes while with TBWA Singapore, where he helped the agency win its first ever two Gold Lions, lifting them to number one in the market, as well as earning five local and regional Agency of the Year citations.

Working with some amazing talent throughout the network's 17 offices, Y&R Asia has experienced a creative resurgence in the last two years. Y&R Jakarta won the country of Indonesia it's first ever Gold Lion in 2010 and Y&R Singapore won Republic of Singapore Navy after the client being with Saatchi & Saatchi for 28 years – just one the many new business wins in the last three years. The network also has two Guinness World Records under its belt for clients. This year Y&R Thailand won it's first ever Gold Cannes Lion, two for that matter; another first after more than 20+ years for Y&R Thailand.

Marcus Rebeschini, My Thoughts

I don't know Marcus very well. I don't even know him well. But I do know that when I grow up I too, would like to be a CCO Asia. For anyone. Talk about titles. The only one better than that is Grand Panjandrum Asia.

But Marcus deserves both. As you'll read in his bio, he's won so many awards for his Y&R agency group since he's come aboard that they're thinking of changing the name to Young & Rebecam. Nice ring to it.

When I first contacted Marcus about a top position years ago, he had just accepted another important position. And when I contacted him a few years later, wouldn't ya know it, he had just signed on for his Asian sojourn. Talk about ships in the night. Literally.

He was so excited, I was so envious. Not that New York is a backwater. But being based in Singapore. How cool is Singapore?

You look at Marcus' work and you immediately get it. It's all laid out right there. He has the incredible fortune of having an intense insight gene crossed with one of the most subtly obtuse senses of humor you'll ever come in contact with. So he's been the catalyst for writers and art directors all over Asia to aspire to subtle obtusety (don't look it up, I just made it up).

But when you read his story, you'll really understand Marcus. And you may very well say, "That's the kind of person I want to work for."

And if you're subtly obtuse enough, who knows?

My First Time
By Marcus Rebeschini

It's kind of amazing to me how much currency the uber-glamorous days of advertising are getting around the world. Imagine, the phrase Mad Men now automatically means advertising in a specific time and place in most parts of the world. For me it conjures up 1970's and 80's images of 4-hour-long lunches, bright fluorescent coloured Ferraris and Porsches filling up agency carparks and men with well-groomed ponytails.

My own particular exposure to those days began in my own home, growing up with a dad in advertising who always seemed to me to be paid just to have fun. In truth, his first career was more like the Sopranos than Mad Men, and he was not one for ponytails, but by the time I'd come around, he had his own agency and he was whom I looked up to as my father, best mate, mentor and hero.

And he thought it was a grand idea for me to follow his footsteps, so of course I was impressionable enough to do so. (My own idea was to be a car salesman so I could have all the latest and greatest fluorescent coloured Ferraris and Porsches).

My first taste of advertising was via the first ad I produced which was unbeknownst and uncredited to me. I'd done an ad for advertising school for one of the agencies that came to brief us on Yellow Pages. I came up with an idea called "Yellow Brick Road" and submitted a sketch which my teacher passed on to the agency. I'd told my father about my idea before presenting it, so when he was flipping through a magazine and saw it produced, he showed it to me. To make a long story short, the teacher said, "Just goes to show you can do great ideas that will get recognized internationally." (As it won Gold at every show) So that became a turning point for me — doing ideas that people noticed.

I was definitely drawn to my father's lifestyle and the taste of getting more great work out. But I didn't start off driving a lime green 911 porsche; instead, I started off in the world of catalogues. Not just any old catalogue work but arguably the dullest category on the planet – hardware. This under-glamorous world taught me a lot of lessons that have served me well during my career in advertising.

I learnt that there's nothing to lose by pushing the boundaries, I wanted people to talk about my ideas or in this case catalogues.

I changed the templates, experimented with the formats, and basically strove to do the best work I could - despite the brief's apparent lack of creative potential. I wanted the catalogue to be something that if I picked it up I would want to read it and it didn't phase me knowing that my art piece would be read by 100,000 of people why they sat on their toilets and contemplated my masterpieces.

One day my boss came to me & said your idea has just won Gold in a catalogue award show (who knew such a thing existed), but it felt good to know people were noticing my work, something which was nigh on unthinkable for the category and the medium.

Everything can be a lesson in life, a learning. Look around you, see what everyone else is doing then go do the opposite of that. Norms are only norms if you let them be so.

For example look at an advertising annual. Go through it all. Now go back and ask yourself which work did you like? If you can go through the whole book and spot that only a few of the ideas are truly great then you already have a brain that can tell the difference. Now use that power to kill your bad ideas and only keep the great ones. That's what I learnt and why I thought differently on catalogues.

But don't stop there. Look around the world. At your friends. Their kids. Your weird neighbor who keeps training his binoculars on you. And feed your ideas with more than advertising.

And if you can come up with Gold ideas working on hardware catalogues then give me a call, you're just the sort of young creative I'm always looking for.

Kevin Roddy
Chairman/Chief Creative Officer, Riney/SF, Chairman, The One Club

Kevin Roddy recently took over as Chairman and Chief Creative Officer of Publicis & Hal Riney in San Francisco. He is also one of four creative leaders on the Global Creative Board of Publicis Worldwide.

Kevin's approach to inventive creativity has helped him lead prior agencies like BBH, Fallon and Cliff Freeman, to new and broader creative territories. The result of which have included traditional awards as well as awards for innovation like the Cannes Titanium Lion, the AICP NEXT Award (four times), the first-ever AAAA's O'Toole Box Award, and many others. In addition, under Kevin's leadership BBH was named the "AAAA's Mid-Sized Agency of the Year" four years in a row.

As a copywriter Kevin has, himself, been recognized for creative excellence throughout his career. Twice he has been ranked in the top three of *Boards Magazine's* "Top 10 Copywriters Worldwide" list, and he has won every major creative award in the world several times over. In fact, Kevin is the only person in advertising history to have ever won The One Show's "Best of Show" award, twice.In addition to his role at Riney, Kevin currently has the proud honor of being Chairman of The One Club, the advertising industry's most prestigious international club dedicated to championing creativity in all its forms.

Kevin Roddy, My Thoughts

Let me tell you about the kind of person Kevin is. He was CCO of BBH/NY, one of the most prestigious creative shops in the city, if not in the country.

Obviously, he's busy. Super busy. Monumentally busy. Orgasmically busy. So he wouldn't even have time to blow his nose.

So what do I do, knowing that Kevin can't spare a moment to inhale or exhale? I ask for a favor. Not for me; I never do that. But for my son.

My son, Kevin (a happy coincidence that), still in college, was building his CW site and needed some guidance. Well, who better to turn to than his tecayo (name double en espanol)?

And what does Mr. Roddy do? Does he hang up the phone? Does he curse me from Battery Park to Nova Scotia? Does he hire some goons to blow up my car (well, he *did* think about that for a while)?

Nope. He sends Kevin a two page, single-spaced review of his site with suggestions.

That's Mr. Kevin Roddy.

My First Time
By Kevin Roddy

Being a young creative in this business can be a lot of pressure. At least it was for me because my sights were set so incredibly high. The only thing I was ever interested in was creating a fame-launching, award-collecting idea that would put my career in the chair of a rocket sled and blast me, cheeks flapping, to Mach 8 of the advertising industry.

I was lucky in that my hard work and never-say-die approach to finding that Holy Grail caught some wind a couple of copywriting jobs into my career when I found myself on the phone with Cliff Freeman. I don't actually remember a single word of the conversation, but I'm pretty sure he said something about a job.

And the next thing I knew, there I was, sitting on my launch pad—Cliff Freeman & Partners. And the pressure was on from the moment I stepped in the office on my first day, walked up to the receptionist, stuck out my hand to introduce myself and knocked her scalding-hot coffee into her lap. The worst part, though, wasn't that I'd spilled 185-degree coffee in the receptionist's lap but that I'd spilled coffee on one of Cliff's antique Stickley tables that was being used as the reception desk.

Not a great first impression. I think Cliff's wife, Susan, wanted me fired on the spot, but Cliff stuck up for me.

Anyway, early on, I got an assignment for Ameritech Cellular. It was a brief about how good their call quality was. And as was customary at CF&P, it was a "gangbang" with multiple teams—far more talented and heavily awarded teams, at that—all looking to be the one to crack it. Luckily, my partners and I did.

Personally, I loved the idea we sold. Truly loved it. I thought we'd really created something that would make us famous. I was looking up tuxedo rentals in the *Yellow Pages* (the actual *Yellow Pages*, by the way—a thick book filled with real paper pages because, well, at that time there wasn't an app for that) and writing my acceptance speech on a cocktail napkin before we even went into production.

The first step toward tragedy, however, came on a director's call. I won't name the director because, honestly, he's better than this. He was a guy who, at the time, was just getting his start and, frankly, none of us were all that psyched about him as an option. But our producer pushed hard, so we agreed to get on a call and hear what he had to say.

I remember that I was in a radio session for the call. So I was literally dividing my attention between talking to an actor in the booth and talking to the director on the phone.

And it was in this context that I made Mistake #1: people will blow smoke up your underwear to get a job ... don't fall for it. Hire people based on their thinking, their ideas, not their ability to massage your ego—even if it comes with a happy ending.

I've since learned from that mistake and tried to pass on the lesson as best I can, but back then I was young and hungry and, well, gullible, so I fell for it. On the call, the director said something that was music to my inexperienced, impressionable, eager ears (as he knew it would be). He said, "I love this idea. And if you let me make it, I know we'll win a Gold Pencil with it!" Cha ching! I thought, this guy gets it. He sees the brilliance in this idea the way I do. And he will help me win the awards that will afford me an awfully nice rented tuxedo.

He was hired. Leading to the second step toward tragedy.

As talented as this director was, and I'm sure still is, back then he had a drug problem (a teeny-weeny detail the producer failed to mention). So, to put it bluntly, his head wasn't in the game. An understatement if I ever wrote one. This guy was all over the place. He was putting more into his nose than the job.

And to add insult to injury, literally in the middle of preproduction, he changed jobs, signing with a different production company. He would, of course, see this production through with the original company, but the tension between him and them now was palpable.

And while the production company was very professional about the situation, they were no longer invested in this director's career. They didn't have the same drive toward ensuring this guy was successful as they did the day before.

All I could think was, man oh man, why me? Why this production? My rented tuxedo was quickly fading into khakis and a well-pressed sport jacket.

The shoot itself didn't get any better because, as was customary at CF&P, a few hundred people got involved in any production that wasn't done by a senior team. Every creative director, senior producer and second cousin's daughter jumped in. And as they added their "this will make it funnier" moments, the spots got worse. The vision I had was quickly deteriorating. Humor that I believed should come from the situation became opportunities for adding slapstick hilarity.

I tried to insert my opinions but got shot down time and again. I was the inexperienced, unfunny kid.

One particularly tragic moment from the shoot (there were a million of them) came during the setup for one scene where we were shooting from the hood into the front seat of a car, listening to people talking. As I was sitting in video village watching them prep the car for the scene, I saw that they were taking the windshield out. I didn't understand why they would do that, so I went up to the director and DP to ask.

Now it's important to note that the DP wasn't just any DP. He was a two-time Academy Award–winning cinematographer (name withheld to protect the guilty) with a pile of credentials and accomplishments that could keep a peon like me in my box.

I asked them why they would take out the windshield—we were shooting at night, and the way the shot was framed, it would look like there was no windshield in the car. Both the director and the Academy Award winner looked at me like I was a silly, inexperienced, thumb-sucking child. They practically laughed at me and told me it was the right way to do it. I was dismissed without so much as a discussion.

As I walked back to video village, all I could do was think that they must know what they were doing. So I let it go.

Big mistake. It wasn't until I was sitting in the edit suite a week later, looking at that scene—and seeing what looked like a car driving down the street without a windshield—that I'd wished I'd stuck to my guns.

It's important to remember that, just because someone is a supposed expert, it doesn't mean they're always right. Trust your gut. Question things. Don't be stupid and think you know it all but also don't accept their opinion on its face just because they say so. Insist that they help ou understand what they're saying. It's a great way to ensure you get it right—this time and the next.

This shoot was, for a whole host of perfect-storm reasons, a calamity. Our great, fame-launching idea ended up as nothing more than an embarrassing pimple in the middle of my forehead. The campaign was a Frankenstein's monster of what I'd imagined it to be ... and a drug-damaged monster at that.

And my tuxedo, well, it was never more than a T-shirt ... wrinkled with sweat stains in the pits.

The funny thing is, recently a different phone company produced an incredibly similar (that's a kind way of saying "identical") idea. I won't name the phone company or the agency, but I will say that they did a far better job producing it than we ever did. And you know what? It won a ton of awards. Pencils, Lions and lots of sparkly, metal objects that sit on somebody's bookshelf collecting dust and a whole lot of jealousy. Not the least of which is from me.

I learned a lot from that fiasco. The most important thing being that an idea that comes out of my noodle must be mine. I need to own it. I need to listen and be open to other ideas, but, if I don't believe they are making my idea better, I need to put my foot down. And occasionally that means I need to wear steel-shank boots.

I must admit, I love advertising. I really do. But there are times when it doesn't seem to love me—hell, it doesn't seem to even enjoy my company. But I keep trying. Keep looking for those tuxedo-renting ideas. Because without those, I'm just another poorly dressed copywriter with an acceptance speech at the bottom of his drawer next to his unfinished screenplay.

William Rosen
Consulting Partner, VSA Partners

Prior to beginning his engagement with VSA Partners leading its consumer marketing practice, William was president and chief creative officer of North America for Arc Worldwide, the global marketing company and part of Leo Burnett Worldwide and the Publicis Group. He was responsible for the strategic and creative product across all disciplines — digital, direct/CRM, promotion and shopper/retail marketing — for clients including McDonald's, Procter & Gamble, Coca-Cola, Nestlé Purina, Comcast, Walgreens, United Airlines, Whirlpool and MillerCoors.

William took the top creative spot at Arc Worldwide in 2004, when Frankel, a leading marketing agency he headed as chief creative officer, merged into Arc Worldwide. There his team was recognized more than 300 times with major creative awards and rankings around the world including the Oracle World Retail Award's "Retail Advertising Campaign of the Year" and the MAA Worldwide Globes "Best of the Best in the World," as well as awards for "Best New Media," "Best Multidiscipline Campaign," several "Best in Show" awards, and three Lions at the Cannes International Advertising Festival. William served as president of the jury at the Cannes Lions International Advertising Festival, as well as at the Spikes Asia Advertising Festival, and has served on juries for the Clio Awards, the Effie Awards, the London International Advertising Awards and numerous other leading industry award shows.

Bill Rosen, My Thoughts

When I first met Bill, he was CCO of the ARC division of Leo Burnett. Then he also became president. Wow! Here's a guy who must be doing something right. Or he has an identical twin, each doing his own thing.

For some reason, Bill reminds me of when I was a little boy and my mother would take me to a kindly doctor. The doctor would seat me down, playfully tussle my hair, look down at me and say: "Well, now. Tell me where it hurts and we'll fix it."

I just can't get that doctor image out of my mind whenever I think of Bill.

I guess, in a way, he is a kindly doctor, saying the same thing to clients and the people he works with, and the people who work for him.

To say that he's been incredibly successful in his area of expertise (integrated shopper marketing) would be like saying Babe Ruth was a good hitter. And judging from Bill and his pitch/win ratio, I think his B.A. might even be higher than the Bambino's.

Here's a guy who judges at Cannes, writes for the Harvard Review, flies all over the world for his clients, and still finds time for a Big Mac.

Back to WOW!

My First Time
By William Rosen

My first time working on a major national marketing campaign took place in the late Mesozoic period. Our creative team had just survived the second mass extinction of the dinosaurs, and we were beginning work on a national program leveraging McDonald's sponsorship of the upcoming Tim Burton film, "Batman Returns." That was the installment starring Danny DeVito, Michelle Pfeiffer and Michael Keaton (remember Michael Keaton? …).

I was a young, recently hired writer, partnered with an amazing, veteran art director named Dave Kopera, who happened to be a comic book collector. He was a fabulous partner, who recognized, as I did, that we had a unique opportunity to do something unprecedented with this exciting collaboration between two mega-brands.

Dave and I set to work developing concepts that would connect the brands and draft off the movie hype to benefit our client. Dave's first-hand insight into the world of Batman and its most fervent fans was nothing short of enlightening. It helped me begin to understand and appreciate the depth and breadth of the passion these collectors had for their subjects. It also led to our first epiphany, namely that anything and everything associated with the franchises collectors love was worth collecting, and as a result, had both emotional and monetary value.

We followed that thinking with what would best be described as a reverse product placement idea. We seized on one of the Batmobile's obscure weapons that was very briefly (and completely insignificantly) mentioned in the script – a small metal disc that was fired out of the front of the car. We turned it into an exclusive flying "Bat Disc" that McDonald's customers would receive as a special lid on their drink cups. It was a movie prop come to life, and we knew collectors would go crazy for it … as would any tween or teen who dreamed of launching projectiles at real or perceived enemies just like their hero Batman.

If the thinking had stopped there, we would have had a solid, but unremarkable, promotional tie in. What I believe made this program so successful, and so ahead of its time, was that we took the approach that every piece of communication should be viewed as collectable … including the McDonald's fry box. That's right … We proposed altering the then sacrosanct brand icon, the red and gold McDonald's fry box, to a sleek bat black.

Black was not the first color that came to mind when you thought of family-friendly McDonald's. Nor was a big Batman logo on the front of French fry box. But we understood that this six-week alteration to a brand icon would capture attention, and the imagination of collectors. Unfortunately, our idea was shot down not once, not twice, but three times by our clients. It was obvious why. The red and gold fry box was a brand treasure that any competitor would kill for, and to change it, especially back in the Mesozoic period, was sheer blasphemy. Secondly, we were proposing the anti-family-friendly color of black, and the logo of one of the most tortured "heroes" in comic book history. That was precisely the point, of course. Our creative brief said to turn this sponsorship into a real "event," and we knew that this kind of shake-up would do just that.

Obviously we eventually convinced our visionary and wisely cautious clients to make the change (or I wouldn't be telling the story now), and CNN covered it as news. Suddenly everyone was talking about this first-ever alteration to McDonald's famous icon and "event" status had been achieved even before launch.

Fans and devotees of both McDonald's and Batman went on to collect thousands of greasy fry boxes (each with the visage of a different film character on the back) in addition to their Bat Discs, driving results that made this one of McDonald's most successful teen and young adult programs to date.

We managed to penetrate the cultural zeitgeist a second way, if you'll excuse the expression, when a major magazine wrote a full page article about the size of the codpiece on the Batman standee that greeted visitors at McDonald's. Apparently, the author believed, Batman was a bit too well endowed. We had "scaled" him back a touch once, but apparently not far enough (or just far enough, depending on your perspective). He's a super hero, after all, we figured, having no idea we'd create even more buzz for the program.

The lessons were clear and broadly applicable to future opportunities. Base your ideas on real insights into the people you want to engage. Dare to push the boundaries. Persevere ... and, of course, never underestimate the power of a well proportioned codpiece.

Marshall Ross
Executive Vice President, Chief Creative Officer, Cramer-Krasselt

Marshall is bald and allergic to everything that tastes good. That ought to say it all. But for the record, he joined C-K in 1995, and was part of the agency team (which includes many of the people you're reading about today) that steered C-K to being the second largest independent in the country, garnering everything from multiple Effies to the Cannes Lion.

In his life before C-K, Marshall was a copywriter and creative supervisor at Foote, Cone & Belding. At the age of 27, he had the thoroughly naive idea of starting a creative boutique in a large agency town. To most everyone's surprise, Mitchiner, Ross & Kahn managed a successful six-year run in Chicago before being acquired in 1992 by Campbell Mithun Esty, where Marshall assumed the post of executive creative director.

His account experience includes all of C-K's accounts and McDonald's, 7UP, Coors Beer, Payless Shoes, Citibank and several campaigns for The Partnership for a Drug-Free America. He also collaborated with filmmaker John Hughes on a picture that absolutely defines the word "flop." Marshall's hobby is work. Other interests include worrying and germ avoidance.

Marshall Ross, My Thoughts

"Get outta town, Ringo! Marshall Ross is a comin'!"

Imagine a CCO with a midnight-black ten gallon hat pulled down menacingly over one eye, two multi-notched six-shooters slung low over his muscular, slender hip, his black leather vest and saddle-worn jeans dusty from the sagebrush and desert sand, striding into a client's conference room, putting one scruff- booted leg up on the chairman's chair, lifting an unlit cheroot from his lizard-like lips, spitting, as he snake-smiling says: "So I guess you just approved our proposal. Pard!"

Well, that wouldn't be *our* Marshall Ross. Nope. Our Marshall Ross is about as un-martial as you can get. He cries when kittens are stuck up a tree. His sense of humor is so jaundiced, doctors keep giving him quinine pills. He's so slim that if he turns sideways in a meeting, people think he's left the room.

But the funny thing is, so I've heard, that when Marshall is presenting to a client or a prospective one, he becomes that dominating, center-of-gravity person like his wild west doppelganger. Without the spitting or Colt .45s.

I've heard stories where his performance during one of these presentations was so compelling that Elmer Gantry took notes.

This is the mild-mannered man who's the CCO and partner of the largest, privately held, multi-office agency in the U.S., with close to 200 creatives reporting to him, scattered around four offices, and he doesn't even wear a badge. Just a smile.

But then again, when you're "Marshall Ross", all the bad creative folk skedaddle when ya ride into town.

My First Time
By Marshall Ross

My First F-You.

Like many First Time stories, mine involves humiliation.

First, let's get the record straight on the notion of "first time." In a business as dynamic and fast paced as advertising, the first times never stop coming. There's the first time you get a job in advertising. Then the first time you quit a job because like most first jobs in advertising, yours requires taking direction from a committed drunk. There's the first time you present to a room full of people and learn why in 1967 scientists added a chemical cocktail called antiperspirant to deodorant. This is followed immediately by the first time you understand the limits of science. There's the first time a junior client with fewer brain cells than asparagus kills a great idea because the company he's been at for a full three months now, "… just doesn't like humor. Cheese, you know, is a serious business." There's the first time you take a late-night drive out to the Federal Express office at the airport because you missed the last pick up of the evening and your first time sending work over the Internet is still eight years in the future. This coincides with your first time meeting the Federal Express employees who don't normally engage in customer service or pass their drug tests.

Ad people spend a lot of time in airports so plenty of first times happen there. Like the first time you sleep on a cot at the Dallas/Fort Worth airport because American Airlines lied (not for the first time) that your plane would soon be here. There's the first time you learn how stupid it is to discuss pitch strategy on a crowded plane. There's the first time someone rips one louder than a 737 taking off during a tense presentation to a client CEO. Sorry, that didn't really count as an airport story, but it's true and I think the 737 reference makes it work.

Switching subjects without grace, who can forget the first time you witness what happens when an over-worked art director falls asleep with an unopened can of soup heating up on a hot plate? That creates the kind of screaming

192

only a typo on the cover of a very expensive catalog inspires when it's discovered for the first time. After being reproduced in ink 1.7 million times.

My point is, while this story takes place in my relative youth and inexperience, this wasn't technically my first ad or my first job. It was though during my first days at a *new* job, an important detail I like to think explains the tragedy about to unfold.

My Group Creative Director at Foote Cone & Belding, now called Draft FCB and not the first time an ad agency moniker would go from bad to worse, asked me to supervise the production of a radio script he had written. This was perilous on several fronts.

Front one: Unless it meant tuning in a station, I was in no position to supervise anything with the word radio in front of it. All my previous and brief experience was in print. Front two: It was my BOSS' script. Front three: It was my NEW BOSS' script. A producer by the name of Ron Nelkin was dispatched to help me through my first time. Out of respect to Ron, I'll change his name in this story to Ron Nelkin. Ron was good at many things, but caring much about how a rookie copywriter was doing at producing his BOSS' radio script was not one of them. Ron introduced me to the studio staff and went to lunch for the next three days.

I was left alone to "direct" the casting session. Casting, most people understand, is one of the most important starts to a great spot, second only to the idea itself. But when it's your First Time, you are not most people. You are considerably dumber. This was in Chicago during the early '80's. It was a time when some really great comics were making names for themselves at Second City. They all liked to do ads, too, because The Second City didn't pay with anything you could also call money. One of those comedians was Dan Castellaneta. You know him better as the voice of Homer Simpson, and a half dozen other characters on the show. I was young and the Simpsons thing hadn't really blown up yet, and so maybe I could be forgiven for insulting Dan Castellaneta during the audition. But Dan didn't think so. To the best of my recollection, here's what happened:

Dan did something really funny and great with the script. Meaning he changed it. To make it actually funny versus something that merely aspired to be funny, he improvised much of it on the spot. And even though I laughed, and even though the engineer laughed (a rare occurrence I would later learn), and even though I knew that Dan had been on TV in some vague way and likely knew funny better than I did, all I could hear were the last words my GCD had said just after he handed me THE SCRIPT HE WROTE, "Go make this spot for me. Don't screw it up." So naturally my smart and experienced response to a person that would soon be known as one of the best and funniest voice actors in all of human history was ... "Hey, how about we stick to the script, okay?"

That was the day I received my first, "You don't know what the fuck you're doing, do you, *Fuckhead*?"

There's something about the first time someone destined for greatness makes it abundantly clear that as far as he's concerned ... you are not. It's special.

Ted Royer
Partner/ECD, Droga5/NY

Originally from Philadelphia, Ted is currently partner/ECD at Droga5 in NY. Ted graduated from the Portfolio Center in 1995. He won more One Show pencils than anyone in history in his first year as an art director at Leonard/Monahan. While in Saatchi Singapore he was ranked the number 8, and then the number 4 creative in Asia by Campaign Brief. Saatchi was voted the Ad Age International Agency of the Year. While regional CD in Latin America, he was on the Ogilvy & Mather Creative Council, the youngest person ever to be in that group. At Wieden + Kennedy his SportCenter ads became part of a class taught at Harvard about successful business relationships, the example being Wieden and ESPN's fruitful 10 year partnership. He's very proud that his ads were being shown at Harvard, a school he could have never gotten into. At Publicis, Ted was on the Worldwide Creative Council. He ran the Sydney office or a year and then went to NY to make ads for Heineken.

Since his time helping to build Droga5 from it's founding, the agency has been named Creativity's Agency of the year, and has also won impressive awards such as 4 Cannes Titaniums, 4 Cannes Grand Prixes, and two D&AD black pencils in one year. Ted helped win Puma, Method, Activision, Rhapsody. Coke, New Museum, and Net10. Among his nearly 100 international awards are 16 Cannes Lions (including 2 Titaniums), 18 One show pencils, 2 gold Clios and 2 gold Andys. And this year, Creativity ranked Ted as one of the Top Ten Creative Directors in the world for 2011.

Ted Royer, My Thoughts

Before you read Ted's story, please, sit down, take a deep breath and get ready for a happy ride and a primer on handling a prima donna.

By the time I first contacted Ted, he was already *the* Ted Royer. Which was a big deal because he never wanted to be *that* Ted Royer.

Whenever I would call Ted for an important position out of New York City, his response was always a quiet "Whaddayaf**ck*ncrazy?!", or some such genteel response.

It got to the point where I thought he was having a bizarre sexual affair with the Statue of Liberty or a phallic fixation with the Empire State Building.

He once emailed that he'd call when he was back from Bangkok! Bangkok? This from a guy who has port partum blues if he goes to New Jersey!

Or he would tell me that the positions I was contacting him about were too similar to the one he had. Which struck me as odd since one time I called about becoming the emperor of a tiny nation in the middle of the Indian Ocean.

But the thing you come away with from Ted, is his absolute joy of life in general and the creative life of advertising, in particular. I can never remember one time that the work he had done didn't make you smile or laugh or think or just feel good.

And except for dispensing a magical love potion to every conceivable consumer in America, what more could you ask for?

My First Time
By Ted Royer

You are a kid. You watch TV. You watch A LOT of TV. You grow up. More TV. You go to college. You study history. You watch more TV. You graduate. You realize you're not going to get a job because you have a history degree. You watch more TV and think what about what you can do with your life.

Then, as you're watching TV, a Little Caesar's Pizza-Pizza commercial comes on. You realize you want to make that. You realize you probably can make that. You go to ad school (all the while constantly watching TV, because now you can call it research). You get a job.

And that's how I found myself working for David Baldwin at Leonard/Monahan in 1995. David had been kind enough to offer me a job, partly because he liked my book, but mostly, I suspect, because I had Jack Kirby drawings in my resume.

I got an office. I got to work with Kara Goodrich, Greg Bokor, Rob Rich and John Simpson. I laughed a lot. I disliked Providence. I got to know Tom Monahan. I smoked weed. I watched TV.

And I wondered if and when I would be found out.

This was a little ridiculous. I wasn't really an art director. Doing campaigns in school was easy. You thought of a joke, slapped a product on it, and you were good. But at L/M, people were not only nailing difficult briefs, they were crafting the shit out of things. There would be hallway discussions about kerning a line that would last 30 minutes. These people were anal. And they were really, really good. I had tricked them this far, but the time was coming when I would have to show up and perform. And I didn't know if I could or not.

Polaroid was a big, important client of ours. Not only did it keep the lights on, but it allowed the agency to do tons of award-winning work. Kara and Rob had concepted a campaign, but before it got produced, Rob left. There was no one else who could cover it.

It was my first shoot. They flew me to Minneapolis to shoot three print ads. I was warned the client loved to be involved, and that this particular client was "a bit of a starfucker". It would be very important to her to know that one of our very best creatives was running the shoot. Even though this was my first shoot ever, I was instructed to act as if I knew EXACTLY what I was doing at all times.

We get to the shoot and begin to set up. All seems cool. I talk with the photographer and he's great, really open. The sets look good. Then the client walks in. Instantly she was the center of attention. The account guy fell over himself laughing at her jokes. It was the first time I had seen how an agency lives in low-level fear of the client. It was so new to me. Everyone's anxiety only served to increase my own. I wasn't too nervous to begin with, but watching everyone else get nervous made me nervous.

We started going over the shots. She asked some typical client questions, and made typical client comments. Then. When we were looking at one framing for a shot, she turned to me and said, "The lighting looks strange, we can't see the model, it's so dark, how do you intend to fix that?"

The whole table went silent and turned to look at me. I was on the spot. No one else could field the question because it had been specifically addressed to me. It was mine and mine alone. I needed a strong answer, and I needed that answer to come out quickly. Every millisecond I hesitated would blow my cover, would reveal that I didn't have any business running a print shoot for one of the most well-known brands in the country. How much money had they put into this shoot? How much had it cost to fly me up here? How much was my hotel room? What was the agency's fee for this job? All of it, ALL OF IT seemed to be jeopardized by my hesitation.

If my answer sucked, it would show everyone I didn't belong here. There would be phone calls, complaints that the agency had sent some inexperienced dolt to run things. I might get fired. Worse, I might get the agency fired.

Fuck it. I couldn't fake my way through this. I didn't care about impressing this woman. I cared about becoming the person that actually does this job.

I said "We increase the light behind her to silhouette her head, then we put a soft light on her face. The background light will frame her but the front light will allow us to see her expression."

Thankfully, my art director brain had overridden my client ass-kissing brain and I had actually answered with a real solution, not a bullshit one. And it was an eye-opening moment. So what if I had never done this before? So what if this was my first shoot? I had trained for it, I had a passion for it, and I had earned the right to take a stab at this project, right now. If not me, who?

My answer made her smile. Its real confidence had won her over. I didn't have to fake it. The shoot turned out great. The campaign won One Show pencils. And I became an art director.

If not you, who?

Glen Schofield
CEO, Co-Founder, SLEDGEHAMMER GAMES, Executive Producer, "Call of Duty"

Glen A. Schofield has been in the video game industry for over 22 years and has worked on over 50 games and have grossed over $3.5 Billion dollars. His last game, which he co-directed, was *Call of Duty: Modern Warfare 3*, is the largest selling Entertainment property in history having passed the $1 Billion dollar mark in only 16 days. *MW3* has won dozens of awards worldwide including the coveted Academy of Interactive Arts and Sciences (AIAS) "Best Action Game" for 2011. Glen's previous game, which he created, was *Dead Space* for Electronic Arts also won the AIAS "Best Action Game" for 2009. Currently he is the CEO of Sledgehammer Games, an Activision/Blizzard Studio he co-founded in 2009. Glen has been a Vice President at Crystal Dynamics and Electronic Arts as well as Activision Blizzard. His games have won countless awards including the *British Academy of Film and Television Arts (BAFTA's), Spike TV's Video Game Awards, AIAS, G.A.N.G. Awards* and many others. He has been on the Late Night with Jimmy Fallon Show, G4 X-Play Show, IGN's Up at Noon, Spike TV, and spoken at the Microsoft Press Event at E3, the Orpheum Theater, Stanford University, SF Academy of Fine Arts and many others. He has traveled throughout the world and recently spoke and conducted interviews in Tokyo, Paris, Madrid, Berlin, Cologne, London, Milan, Stockholm, etc. His many games include: MW3, Dead Space, Lord of the Rings, James Bond, Blood Omen 2, Knockout Kings, The Simpsons, Godfather, Ren and Stimpy, Gex 2 and 3, Goofy, Swamp Thing, Disney World racing and many others. He currently lives in California with his wife Barbara and three children.

Glen Schofield, My Thoughts

I've known Glen for over 20 years. Longer than anyone else in this book.

I knew Glen before he moved to California and became *"the"* Glen Scbofield; the exec producer of the biggest selling video game in history.

I knew Glen when he and I worked on a very funny, bizarre kind of comic strip, sort of a *Far Side* with a kids' slant (we still may sell it one day). Kids right out of *Village of the Damned*.

I knew Glen as one of the best, most out-there illustrators you would ever hope to meet and work with.

And after all this time, all his success, all the awards, all the adulation, he's still one of the kindest, most hard-working, passionate people in the business.

I *know* this because we've remained friends for all of these years and because we've just completed the first in a series of children's books together; but nothing like the nest of little monsters we created before.

Though we have one central character in this series, an important lesson is taught in each book.

And I just thought of another important lesson to be taught: have a friend like Glen and twenty-plus years go by very, very quickly.

My First Time
By Glen Schofield

I got my first break in videogames in 1991. The industry was pretty small back then and no one really knew if it was a fad or not and how long it would be around. I didn't care because it was an opportunity to use computers, create art and work in a cool studio. I had established myself somewhat as a freelance artist in the late '80's but I wanted a full time job as I was engaged and ready to get married. A friend of mine was working at a small videogame company called Absolute Entertainment. They brought me in and had me "test" my skills for a week without pay. I then waited about three weeks before I finally received the call that the job of videogame artist was mine. I think I was the 17th employee with about 8 artists on staff already, all very talented.

They had some great games I was excited to work on: Swamp Thing, The Simpsons, Ren and Stimpy, a War Game, etc. But I was the new guy and I didn't get to choose. There was one game nobody wanted so, of course, it was given to me. The game was Barbie Game Girl to be created in four shades of gray/green. Just great. Here I am a weight lifting, semi-tough guy from New Jersey and I get Barbie (no offense). I couldn't even tell my parents since my dad was an even tougher guy working in construction. It was bad enough I was an artist (although my parents supported me 100%), but Barbie? All the artists had a great time with it- leaving purses and Barbie Dolls on my desk and sending me all kinds of "reference" material. At least they were enjoying it.

I decided I would dive into it with everything I had. I was the new guy and I needed to show them they picked the right person. I had something to prove and, to be honest I didn't mind because I was designing and creating art. I studied Barbie, women's clothes, shoes, flowers, haircuts and accessories. I had all the latest women's magazines piled all over my area. I taped up pictures of my favorite outfits and accessories. Actually, I started worrying about myself. Plus, of course, Barbie went to salons, clothing stores, lingerie boutiques, flower shops and just about every other place I knew nothing about. I was creating new hair styles, high heeled shoes, dresses, whatever. I went to lingerie stores, salons, women's clothing stores, you name it. I even considered getting a waxing (just for a minute!) There were no explosions, aliens, guns, badguys, lava, monsters or anything that I considered cool, but I put everything I had into it. All along I heard every joke and wisecrack you can imagine. I tried to be the Teflon artist and have none of it stick to me. I was immersed in everything feminine for almost four months. I knew my stuff and became a Barbie expert. The guys almost went too far when they started calling me Ken instead of Glen. Or they'd change a Barbie ad or box to say "Barbie and Glen". So I did what we do in Jersey, if anyone bothered me I just threatened to crush them or challenged them to arm wrestling competitions. That seemed to work...for a while. I could still see them pointing, whispering and laughing from across the studio.

After four months I was done. Barbie looked great, had the latest fashions and visited all the coolest women's places. I was really proud of the final product. That still didn't stop the jokes and little gifts and flower baskets from appearing on my desk. But my new bosses and, more importantly, the client were extremely happy. It turned out better than anyone expected.

Finally the game came out. It was a hit! People forgot how big Barbie was and that everything with Barbie on it's cover sold like crazy. It out sold all our other games by a pretty big margin. The joking finally stopped. I think the guys were a little stunned. My bosses took notice of how much I researched the subject, did my job with a smile, worked with the client, took direction, asked questions, won arm wrestling matches and didn't let the joking get me down. Truth is I actually had a good time doing the game and was just thrilled to be coming to work every day to create art. In addition, I was learning the computer, some software packages and a new industry. Little did I realize how huge the industry would become and that Barbie would be the start of a long and fulfilling career.

During this time, the company was also really growing, getting a lot more work and hiring more and more artists. One day the big boss called me into his office. I thought for sure it was to give me the Barbie sequel or some other game that involved hair salons or body waxing. But instead they promoted me to head of the art department! I got the last laugh. Now I was in charge of all the guys who had been laughing at me (in a good way). They were a bunch of great guys and knew their jokes and sketches of me as Ken and me lifting weights in a dress was all in good fun. But they knew that I also would be assigning artists to their projects. Let's just say the I wouldn't be doing the next Barbie game or Hello Kitty. Revenge is sweet. My next game involved monsters, lava, explosions and weapons!

The lesson I learned was no matter what the assignment is, throw yourself into it. Research, become an expert. It's those details that you add that make the product special but also make it enjoyable as the creator. Make the best of it, be passionate and grateful that you're doing something you love, even if the subject matter isn't your first choice. It will show in your work and you never know who will be taking notice.

Mariano Serkin
Co-ECD, Del Camp Saatchi & Saatchi

Mariano Serkin started working in the advertising industry as a copywriter in 1998. In the past 15 years, he's had the pleasure of working in agencies such as BBDO Argentina and Del Campo Saatchi & Saatchi, and in 2007 Mariano Serkin assumed the Executive Creative Direction position at Del Campo.

Throughout his career, Mariano Serkin has been awarded with 31 Lions and 1 Grand Prix from the prestigious Cannes Lions Festival. In the last edition of the Festival, he was recognized as one of the Top 3 most awarded Executive Creative Directors, according to the Cannes Report. During his management at Del Campo Saatchi&Saatchi, the agency was crowned five consecutive years as Agency of the Year by the Circulo de Creativos Argentinos, and Agency of Iberoamérica for two consecutive years at the Festival El Ojo. In 2011, AdAge chose Del Campo as International Agency of the Year. And in 2012 as Creativity Agency A-List.

Mariano Serkin has worked for numerous global and local brands such as InBev, Procter & Gamble, Coca Cola, Cadbury, Milka, Trident, Adidas, Nike, Sony , PlayStation, Sony CyberShot, Zoo de Buenos Aires, Hospital Alemán and the home electrical appliances local brand BGH, among the most prominent.

Mariano Serkin, My Thoughts

It's a bit more difficult for me to give you any sage insights into Mariano as a person because I've never been to Buenos Aires (except listening to the soundtrack of "Evita", but that doesn't count). Or interacted with him on a regular basis over the years. In fact, the first time we spoke was when I called him about "My First Time".

What I can tell you is this, first, he was suggested to me by one of his mutual judges at Cannes who said Mariano was one of the nicest people you'd want to meet.

Well, since I like to meet nice people I emailed Mariano and we spoke. From the first "Buenas tardes", we were old friends. My Spanish was far inferior to his English, but he understood what this book was about, and immediately agreed to become a contributor.

What I got from that and his quick turnaround time in submitting his story is a happy eagerness to be part of the world advertising community and a genuine love of what he does and wants to continue doing.

But the best description of Mariano will come not just from his story, but from his own gentle, fertile creative mind: the samples of his first produced work; which he was kind enough to find and include.

My First Time
By Mariano Serkin

On December 15th, 2002, I started as a Junior Copywriter at the agency Del Campo Saatchi & Saatchi. During that time I lived in a small neighborhood called Villa Luro. Where I used to live is not a minor detail, as the Agency was one hour and a half by bus from home. So to my regular day of work I had to add 3 hours commuting. But to me that was the wonder of my work, because I used that time to think a Brief during the trip.

I still remember to this day those first weeks filled with the inevitable discomfort of being the new one. Don't ask me why, but I always feel uncomfortable being the new one at a work place.

At that time Del Campo Saatchi & Saatchi was an agency that had a few years of life and was trying to show its creative potential to the world; and as every starting agency, it was also trying to develop new business.

One week after I arrived, Chavo and Channel, the Executive Creative Directors then, gathered all the agency's creative teams, and told us the agency was entering the Zoo de Buenos Aires pitch. And the best of it all, we had to present to the client on December 26th, so we had to work during December 24th. Yes of course, during Christmas. We only had one day to think of an outdoor campaign for the Zoo of Buenos Aires. And if there was some time left, spend Christmas with our families.

Now, before continuing this story, let me tell you a bit about the political context and what it was like living in Argentina. Our country was going through one of the biggest economical crisis of its history. The financial system had collapsed and as a result of that, people lost most of their life savings. So thanks God the campaign we had to make was not for a Bank... Within this social framework, the Zoo appeared to be a convenient option for the families to enjoy an entertainment available to all.

That was how, on December 24th, I took my daily bus to the agency and used the time to think about the campaign. I arrived to the agency, locked myself in a box, with Iñaki, my team colleague at that time, and we worked together nonstop. We forgot it was a pitch and worked on the brief as if it was an order to be published. For me that was the opportunity to show the potential we had. Remember I was the new guy!

And that was how we focused on two objectives: the first one was that the campaign worked in a simple way - that with just a glance you could understand it. And the second one: reflecting the value that the Zoo had amid such a social and financial context of the country.

That was how by combining those ingredients we got to a price campaign. We made a rough and presented it that afternoon to Pablo del Campo, the Agency Founder, who after seeing all the work, decided to go to the Client with our campaign.

The rest of the story is a typical and magical Christmas story because with that campaign we won the pitch and published our first work at the agency. Some months after, I remember Pablo del Campo entering my office along with the Saatchi & Saatchi Global Creative Director Bob Isherwood, who was visiting Buenos Aires. Bob looked at my colleague and me and with a smile told us the Zoo de Buenos Aires campaign had won the Ad of The Year of the Saatchi & Saatchi network.

I didn't speak a word of English then, so until Pablo translated the news to me I hadn't understood a single thing. The Zoo de Buenos Aires campaign is until today the most awarded outdoor campaign in the history of Argentina.

So today, almost 10 years later, I still maintain the same discomfort you have when you are the new guy. Because it helps me to keep my desire intact and keeps me always far from the comfort zone; and it is *there* where the ideas live and hit you in the face. And above all, finding the opportunity there is in every brief, even in the ones you have to solve during Christmas.

Here I attach three pieces of the Campaign for you.

Kash Sree
Former CCO, SS+K, New York

Kash was born in Singapore, grew up in the East End of London and has been fortunate enough to have worked in four continents and one sub-continent. Kash switched from art to copy and began a long journey to becoming one the world's most-awarded advertising writers. He was part of the team that helped Batey ads become Asian Agency of the Year in 1995. He then helped DDB Sydney become Campaign Brief's Australian Agency of the Year in 1997.

At Wieden & Kennedy, Portland he spent five years creating some of Nike's most memorable work of the time. Including the Tiger Wood's 'Hackeysack' spot, and the Nike 'Play' campaign. At Leo Burnett Chicago in 2002, graduating from a writer to Creative Director, he helped reposition Nintendo with the "Who Are You?" campaign.

In 2005, he joined BBH, New York as Group Creative Director, successfully helping to globally reposition the ailing Vaseline brand there, with the "Keeping Skin Amazing" campaign. Next came JWT New York as ECD, where he started the process of turning around some very challenging accounts, like Scott Toilet Tissues, Sunsilk Haircare, Kleenex, Visine, and DeBeers. In 2009, Kash became the ECD of an 18 month old start up, Pereira O'Dell. A year later they were Small Agency of the Year. In 2011, he joined SS&K as their CCO. In the next year they increased their billings by 24%, won their first Cannes gold lion and their first One Show pencils in nearly a decade.

Kash and I always seem to be just missing. Since 2000.

Whenever I called, he had just accepted another position. Or the position wasn't right. Or the moon was in the wrong phase. Just one of those silly, little things. It got so that I was afraid if I called him, the Mayans' predictions would come to pass.

Anyway, he's been the top creative at some of the best agencies in the country, and worked at some of the best agencies in the world. And though he lists Chuck McBride and Jim Riswold as two of his greatest influences, he also lists Bruce Lee (although I don't remember him winning anything at Cannes). But he could kick the crap out of Chuck and Jim.

Kash has a rather jaundiced view of life, which is fine, since I share his views (I'm a native New Yorker and you can't get any more jaundiced). His work has turned an ailing elephant into a truly magical, mystical commercial or something as prosaic as toilet paper into an LSD trip with a Daliesque dalliance. Now *that* takes talent. Or LSD.

Another thing I really admire about Kash is his love of family. Having two sons, one daughter-in-law, and the best wife in the world (after 30 years she's either that or the *dumbest* wife in the world), I have a soft spot for family-centric people.

Kash even tells a story about how his young son taught him the simple human joy of tasting raindrops with his tongue.

That's true poetry and love; and jaundice has nothing to do with it.

My First Time
By Kash Sree

This isn't one of those first ads where you'd say "that's a talent to look out for."

I wish it was.

For two months my partner and I had been at Ogilvy & Mather, London, trying to turn a placement into a full time job. Placements were very poorly paid internships. I got 35 pounds a week to cover my expenses. It cost me 50 pounds a week to get to work. This was back in 1991.

The thing with placements is, if you'd been there too long without selling anything, they'd let you go and bring in the next hungry team. Although we had been given a handful of briefs, some of which we'd done good work for, we still hadn't sold anything.

We were getting worried.

Then we got a brief for Lucozade Sport. It was one of the first energy drinks in the UK.

Lucozade ads usually had England's world champion decathlete, Daly Thompson. Head thrown back heroically chugging down the stuff between events.

This stuff was isotonic (that was new back then), the body could absorb it quicker than other drinks. The brief said something like "Lucozade helps you replace all the fluids you've lost on the field." And it came in a revolutionary new squishy foil pack with a spout. Instead of a bottle or a can (that was new back then, too).

Isotonic, we were informed, allowed your body to replenish the fluids you'd lost during sport, more quickly. We thought we had a great line "BLOOD SWEAT AND TEARS REFILL PACK". Our Creative Directors liked it. The account team loved it. The client loved it at first. Then got back to us a day later saying,

"We can't say refill pack. Because they're afraid that since it had a re-sealable spout people could refill it with water."

Seriously.

So we thought about a dehydrated athlete. Completely spent, hunched over a Lucozade Sport, drinking the life replenishing liquid out of its spout with the last of his remaining strength. Above him the line…WHEN YOU'E NOTHING LEFT TO GIVE, TAKE.

Our creative directors loved it. The account team loved it. The client loved it. And still loved it the next day.

We had sold something. We were going to make an ad.

In the next few weeks we got involved in lots of exciting things. Like casting (something we'd never done before), choosing photographers (something we'd never done before), retouching (something we'd never done before). It almost felt like we worked in advertising.

The day before the shoot, the client expressed a concern, " The athlete slumped over like that is too depressing. Can we have him with his head thrown back, downing a Lucozade Sport?" They asked rhetorically. But then the line wouldn't make sense about "have nothing left to give". We protested, meekly. "That's such a great line. It doesn't need the visual saying the same thing." They replied via the account team.

So we changed the visual to the clichéd sports drink pose of the athlete heroically throwing back his head and chugging down sport without squeezing the pack because "then people wouldn't recognize it on the shelf." They had informed us, almost scientifically. "But his bicep wouldn't be flexed if he wasn't squeezing the pack!" we said. "But it looks great." They said. Firmly.

So that's how we shot it. But at least we had a sold ad. Well, not quite. One more change.

"That's a great line but we just need to make a tiny tweak. "Can we make it WHEN YOU'E NOTHING LEFT TO GIVE, TAKE LUCOZADE SPORT?"

And that was my first produced ad. It was quite horrible and in the end it was my fault.

I had forgotten why I had gotten into the business- to make ads that I admired. I had forgotten what many good creatives had warned while I had been doing the rounds.

"Don't show them an ad you're not proud of, because that's the one they'll buy," they had said. I had taken my eye off the ball. I had thought the goal was to get a job and then maybe do great ads, instead of doing great ads to get a job.

I didn't even know how to fight for work back then. But I knew I had to learn. And I probably learned more by doing that horrible ad, than if we'd done a good one.

Rob Strasberg
Co-CEO/Chief Creative Officer, Doner

On Jan. 1, 2010, Rob Strasberg became Co-CEO/Chief Creative Officer and took co-ownership of Doner one of the world's largest Independent advertising agencies.

Rob arrived at Doner in early 2008 from Crispin, Porter & Bogusky in Miami. There he helped create and pioneer a new era of digitally integrated advertising on such signature brands as Truth, Burger King, Sprite, Miller Lite, MINI, and Volkswagen.

Over nine years at CP+B, Rob became one of the "Top Ten Most Awarded Creative Directors in the World" and helped them reach Ad Age's Agency of the Decade. Since joining Doner, he has elevated the agency's integrated portfolio to stand up to the world's best. And under his creative leadership they've won accounts from Chrysler, Dodge, Jeep and Ram to Harmon/JBL, Autozone, Perkins, Choice Hotels, Amazon and Del taco.

He lives in Birmingham, Michigan with his wife Treger and two children. Treger also co-founded the non-profit Humble Design, which helps single mothers in shelters find and furnish a new home. He is very proud of what she does and will brag about it any chance he gets.

Rob Strasberg, My Thoughts

Rob Strasberg had won every award under the sun. And a few under the moon, as well.

He was ECD of Crispin, Porter, Bogusky/Miami and living a balmy life in Miami.

Then I had to go and spoil it all by recruiting him to become the Chief Creative Officer of the world's largest, independent agency, Doner; billing approximately $1.6 billion (yes, that's with a "B").

Now, at the ripe old age of 42, he's not only the CCO, but also Vice Chairman, Co-CEO, and one of two principals. Damn.

Rob is the kind of person you always want to be around. Which presents a problem when he goes home because most of his agency has piled into his car with a mile-long caravan following.

This doesn't phase Rob, but his wife, Treger, finds it trying. Especially at bed time.

Of course I say these nice things about Rob because he totally deserves it. And has nothing to do with the fact that he's hired 4,238 people through me. I wish.

Rob Strasberg
My First Time

My first time is an epic tale of lust, loss and bottled water.

Let me start way back at the beginning. I've wanted to be a copywriter since I was twelve. How is this possible? What twelve year old would ever want to write advertising or even more bizarre, what twelve year old would even know what a copywriter was?

Well, I was fortunate enough to have an Uncle, who was a very, very good copywriter. In fact, he cut his teeth during the golden age of advertising at the goldenest advertising agency of them all, Doyle Dane Bernbach in NYC. My Uncle Marv did famous ads for Volkswagen, Alka Seltzer and American Greeting cards, to name a few. He had an amazing home, a beautiful wife (my Aunt Ellen) and most important he had the respect of our entire family – like a Doctor is respected in normal families.

Thanksgiving '81 was when it happened. That year, besides playing Hide and Seek and cheating my cousins at board games, I found myself in my Uncle's study. I pushed play on his VCR. What I watched for the next 30 minutes was the "Best of" historical reel from Doyle, Dane Bernbach. Or you could say, I watched the birth of modern day advertising. Since that day I wanted to be tested, to see if I could do that, to write truly great ads.

The next day I wrote my first line of copy. My Aunt Ellen notoriously known for bad cooking, so much so that Uncle Marv wrote a very famous ad for Alka-selter commercials about her, was coaxing me into taking out the garbage, "C'mon I'll cook you breakfast" she pleaded. I skidded to a halt in my underoos and replied, "You can't threaten me with your food." I heard a laugh. Uncle Marv was in the room. He smiled. And I was hooked.

Double fast-forward to 1992, I'd landed my first job in advertising. Here's the sad part, I was hired as an Assistant Account Executive – a glorified secretary (I had to take a typing test). And to add to the humiliation it was at DDB Needham (my Uncle hadn't worked there for almost 10 years and by this time "Needham" had joined the masthead). What me worry? I was sure this embarrassing position would only be temporary because I was going to be so funny in the halls that they would surely move me over to the creative department. What I learned very quickly was that if you're trying to be funny in the halls you're not funny, you're annoying.

During one of my non-funny hallway moments I met a girl named Gail. A beautiful girl. She was bright. She was sophisticated. She wanted nothing to do with me. What's a glorified secretary to do? I created reasons to be on her floor. I bumped into her at the cafeteria. I even invited her to the theatre. Nothing. She could tell I was a phony. I wasn't being true to myself.

Enough was enough. Destiny called. I said goodbye to gorgeous Gail. And quit DDB Needham after only a few months and started taking portfolio classes at the School Of Visual Arts. Within a year of night classes and working as a freelance copywriter (I was actually working for free. Zero dollars. Zero assignments. I just watched others work.) I landed my first job at Grace and Rothschild under One Show hall of famers Roy Grace and Diane Rothschild. I couldn't believe it. Then I realized I had to actually produce great ideas. Everyday. I was scared shitless. So shitless in fact that I took up meditating the week before I started.

On my first day, Diane Rothschild and her five shelves of awards, gave me my first assignment - A radio spot for the opening of Origins all natural Bath and Body shop. A radio spot? I'd never written a radio spot. My night classes only covered doing print campaigns. I had 24 hours to come up with something, it seems they'd killed the last two spots sent over by much more seasoned writers than myself and the 15 minutes of experience I had under my belt.

Is it possible to have writers block on your first day? I stayed late into the night determined not to hand in a piece of hack. And then it hit me. I wouldn't write any words at all. I'd create the first radio spot with no words! OK, maybe the name of the store and the day it opened.

I sat across from Diane as she read the first line.

SFX: Twenty seconds of nature sounds – running water, birds chirping, wind rustling the trees, an occasional hawk screech.

223

Then the second line.
VO: (Whispering) Origins, the all natural bath and body shop, is opening a new store at the America Mall January fifth. Please keep it quiet."

She looked up at me and smiled.

A week later I went to my first radio production house. When I walked in the VO announcer was practicing my lines as the engineer was working on the SFX. I was amazed, real people working on something that came from my mind. They both smiled and complimented me on the idea. Crazy.

As I sat back in the big leather couch the engineer asked me if I'd like something to drink – two minutes later who should walk thru the door but Gail. She had left DDB Needham and now worked there. She looked at me and smiled, something she had never done before, as she handed me my bottled water. It might as well have been champagne.

Luke Sullivan
Chair, Advertising Department, Savannah College of Art and Design

After 30 years in the advertising business, author Luke Sullivan is now chair of the advertising department at the Savannah College of Art and Design. He's also the author of the popular advertising book *Hey Whipple, Squeeze This: A Guide to Creating Great Advertising*, and the blog heywhipple.com. His second book releases fall of 2012, titled *Thirty Rooms To Hide In: Insanity, Addiction, and Rock 'n' Roll in the Shadow of the Mayo Clinic.* Sullivan now lives in Savannah with his family. He reports that he "enjoys the indoors" and likes to spend a lot of his time there.

Luke Sullivan, My Thoughts

To say that Luke Sullivan is an advertising Eminence Gris is like saying Babe Ruth was a good hitter.   More importantly, he's a gracious gris. A gris that even shows up in Chris Jacobs' story.

When Luke and I first spoke, he was a CW at Fallon in Minneapolis and he told me he wanted out of the snow. So he moved to an area with little snow; then on to GSD&M in Austin (no snow at all).   And now he's in Savannah, Georgia. He's moved so much that Allied Van Lines wants to change their name to Allied Sulli-Van Lines (couldn't help myself).

But besides being one of the best creatives in the business with a long history of successes, Luke wrote one of the most important, best-selling advertising books of the last two decades: "Hey Whipple, Squeeze This".

It is literally the ultimate advertising guide: anything you want to know is in there: how to create an ad, a TV spot, how to budget them, how to kill the CD who just killed your idea (well, it's not really in there but it should be).

And he's such a dynamic speaker that when I introduced him for speaking gigs to the 4As, they booked him into more venues than Bono.

And now, as you've seen from his bio, he's finally and formally become the teacher he always was. Which teaches us this: keep moving - onward and upward.

My First Time
By Luke Sulivan

A friend of mine, Phil Growick, was writing a book about advertising and he asked me to contribute some thoughts about my earliest experience with the craft, in particular any memories about my "first time," my first successes (or failures).

As many of you know, I am a huge fan of Ray Bradbury. I think he's one of the best writers in captivity. In a biography about the man, Mr. Bradbury remembered the time he first realized he'd written a good short story (The Lake). Of that 1944 story he wrote: "When I finished [writing it], I was crying. I knew at long last, after ten years of trying, I had written something good."

I think as we grow up as artists and creative people, our reach exceeds our grasp for years and years. We grow up being able to see so much more than we can do. We love the creativity we see in the art we love, but it takes years for us to learn a craft well enough to finally make something as good as the things we've been admiring.

So it was with me.

When I first got into the business, my mentors were the Original Minneapolis Duo, Ron Anderson and Tom McElligott. For the first few weeks after they hired me, Ron and Tom put me in a room with their collection of One Show award annuals. They called these books the "graduate school of advertising" and told me to sit down and read them all.

I was such an ad geek that I did more than read them. I Xeroxed every single page of every annual and then cut them all into individual pieces, all the ads, and then assembled all the world's best auto ads in one book, all the best tourism ads in another book, creating a shelf-full of 3-ring binders of the world's best ads broken into categories. Then, whenever I got a job order, whether it was for a restaurant or a brand of liquor, I'd go back to those books and re-read everything in that particular category all over again.

I would give the same advice to students today.

Learning the language of persuasion, of excellent copywriting, it isn't a whole lot different than learning French. It's about immersion. I immersed myself in the craft and you should, too. Eventually all that smart starts to rub off on you.

So I started by copying. I didn't copy concepts of course, but I did my best to copy the rhythms of, say, Neil Drossman's brainy headlines or Ed McCabe's smart-ass writing style. After awhile (in my case it took about 3 years) your own style begins to emerge. You don't decide what your style is, you discover it. Style is hard-wired into your brain and it's a matter of discovering what your style is and then sharpening it, exploring its dimensions.

I'd like to say that once I studied all these masters, my own style quickly emerged and I was brill from then on.

Oh, but becoming good at anything is rarely a graceful process. In those first years, I created some truly horrible things. I've already written about my first ad in my book "Hey Whipple, Squeeze This: A Guide to Creating Great Advertising", and if I may, I'll pull this short quotation:

As hard as I studied those awards annuals, most of the work I did early on wasn't very good. In fact, it stunk. If the truth be known, those early ads of mine were so bad I have to reach for my volume of Edgar Allan Poe to describe them with any accuracy: ". . . a nearly liquid mass of loathsome, detestable putridity."

But don't take my word for it. Here's my very first ad (at the end of my story). Just look at it (for as long as you're able): a dull little idea that doesn't so much revolve around an overused play on the word interest, as it limps.

Rumor has it they're still using this ad at poison control centers to induce vomiting. ("Come on now, Jimmy. We know you ate all of your sister's antidepressant pills and that's why you have to look at Luke's bank ad:

As I said, it ain't pretty and it ain't graceful. I sucked for quite a while and this in spite of having some of the best teachers in the world.

Hall of Famer Tom McElligott once looked at a radio script I presented him, handed it back to me shaking his head and said, "This is a real mess." It was a mess. Oh, it probably had some shred of concept to it but it was undisciplined, not single-minded, it sprawled, it had useless little asides I thought were so clever, and on top of all that, it had the most junior of mistakes -- it didn't time out to a sixty.

I had another excellent teacher, copywriter Dick Thomas. I remember bringing Mr. Thomas another over-long radio spot. He could tell at a glance it was too long and said, "Here, let me just trim it a bit" That's when he fed my script into an oscillating fan he had running on his desk. "There," he said, handing back my shredded, truncated script. "Rewrite it to that length."

May I take a moment here to humbly thank all those brilliant teachers I had early in my career.

And now, in parting, I'll summarize: Study the masters. Immerse yourself in their work over and over again until you have it memorized. Surround yourself with people who are better than you are. Don't waste time defending your early efforts. Just shut up and listen to your teachers. Stay humble. Stay hungry.

Sooner or later you'll produce something that looks like the work you've been studying and admiring. Like Ray Bradbury, one day you'll lean back and realize, wow, all that work, it's starting to pay off.

Carlos Vaca
President, Chief Executive Officer, BBDO Mexico

He started as a copywriter and worked as Creative Director for some of the best international networks like McCann, Lowe and BBDO, where he has been CEO since 2006. Under Carlos leadership, BBDO Mexico won it´s first Cannes Lion in 2008 and more Effie's than any other agency in the country for the last three years. He has attracted some of the most creative and talented teams in the market.

Over the course of his career he has won numerous top local and International awards. He´s passionate about creativity and strongly believes in the powerful results that a Big Idea can produce. He was elected President of the Mexican Creative Circle. He has been board member of the AMAP (Mexican Association of Advertising Agencies) where he was elected President in 2010. He has an active role as a board member in different creative councils. He has had the privilege to serve as jury in many local and International Creative Festival, like FIAP & Ojo de Iberoamerica. He represented Mexico as jury in the past Cannes Lions Advertising Festival 2011.

The Anahuac University recognized him with the "Leadership in Communication" medal in 2009, an honor that has only been awarded five times in 40 years. In addition to advertising, Carlos is passionate about running and Rock & Roll, he has a band in which he plays and sings every Thursday night.

Carlos Vaca, My Thoughts

When I first called Carlos, I spoke to him in my very basic Spanish with English dominating my introduction.

He laughed at my attempts to impress him with my Gringish, then chided me gently by scolding me for not speaking better Spanish. He was right, of course. But I reminded him that I was also illiterate in Yiddish, Italian, German, Russian and Finnish. He laughed again.

But when I told him the idea of "My First Time", I got the biggest laugh of all, with almost the same comment as some of the other contributors: "Can you imagine the crap you're going to get as first ads or commercials? But that is the whole idea, right?"

Of course it is. And when you read Carlos' story, he hits the nail on the head, or "da con en el clavo en la cabeza". Sounds better that way.

What I've learned about Carlos in the few times we've spoken and written to each other, is that he has an incredible sense of humor, an incredible love of advertising, and an incredible desire to be sure that with clients or total strangers like me, "da con el clavo en la cabeza".

My First Time
By Carlos Vaca

During my last year at university, I was working as an editor and writing film critiques in a newspaper. One day I saw a reel with some of the Cannes Lions Advertising Festival winners and at that moment , I decided what I wanted to do for the future.

I knocked at some advertising agencies doors looking for an opportunity as a copywriter but my zero experience made it a difficult task.   After three negatives, I finally went to an interview with a top creative director who I chatted with for an hour or so, demonstrating my passion for films, culture and great advertising. And because of this , I guess I got my first job in the ad industry at Publicidad Ferrer - a local shop which, at that time, was the largest agency in Mexico with a strong creative reputation and an impressive client portfolio.

I was the new kid in town, so no surprise; I was immediately assigned to the accounts that have low, if no, glamour at all. Before I got involved in a campaign, I did all the dirty work that nobody wants in a creative department: like every Friday night checking the copy (proof reader) in all the final arts of a bank account that would be published during the weekend in newspapers (mechanical arts of course, at that time computers were not even a dream).

This was the 80's, and at that time Mexico suffered a terrible economic crisis (the first of many others that we had since then in Latin America). The difficult times caused the agency to make a strong staff reduction in all areas. Surprisingly, I remained in the creative department and was not laid off (I guess because I was the youngest guy in the area and probably the one with the smallest salary).

The agency did a full re-engineering process and I was transferred to another group, the one that handled Domecq, the largest liquors and spirits company in Latin America, at that time. It was there that I wrote the copy for my first ad. The brand was a brandy called Don Pedro, and the selling line was a mandatory: *Don Pedro, el gran Brandy del Don.* This basic and dumb words game meant something like: Don Pedro, the great Brandy of the Gift (El Don).

The Mexican regulations for alcohol advertising are very strict and have many don'ts. Alcohol ads are permitted, but you simply can't show or tell almost anything you could imagine in the story, because you'd be promoting alcohol consumption (which, in essence, is a contradiction).

With this context, and under the close supervision of the Chief Creative Officer, I presented a TV idea that showed an artist working in his studio while making a giant classic sculpture of a man. When he hit the solid rock with the hammer, we hear a voice of saying:

"Donde el arte se vuelve cincel y martillo ahí está el Don.
Don Pedro, el gran Brandy del Don".

The English translation would mean something like:
"Where the art turns Chisel and Hammer, there´s a gift
Don Pedro, the great Brandy of the Gift".

I shared the idea with the CCO and it was selected to be presented to the client. Believe it or not, the client not only liked it but asked for the development of a full campaign of "Fine Arts" for the brand.

The campaign was very successful and the brand indicators grew significantly. It was a great experience, because when someone trusts in you and your talent, amazing things can happen, especially at a young age.

I look today at this ad and find it horrible and cliché, but it worked well not only for the brand, but also for my career.

The next year Jaime Diaz, who was the Chief Creative Officer, resigned to start his own agency and invited me to be a part of his creative project. I didn´t think twice and joined the brand new agency. Unfortunately he passed away two years later, but I always remember him as one of the most inspirational and passionate guys in our business.

Later, some international agency networks contacted me and I continued my creative career in advertising at Lowe and BBDO where I enjoy what I like the most: "Doing great advertising".

Doug Van Andel
Global Creative Director, Saatchi & Saatchi X

An international award-winning Global Creative Director, Doug has partnered with the world's most iconic brands in delivering transformational creative work, engaging clients as they build their business and shoppers on their path to purchase. His unique credentials in digital, experiential, promotions and traditional disciplines, nurtures and directs the creative offerings across Saatchi & Saatchi X's global network in 11 countries.

Doug has over 25 years of experience in virtually every aspect of the ad business and is the perfect mix of right and left-brain creative problem-solving which leads to holistic and impactful campaigns. A native of Southern California, much of Doug's career was with Saatchi & Saatchi LA, witnessing the overwhelming successful global launch of the Toyota Prius and development of Toyota's "Moving Forward" campaign. He has a long track record of award-winning work, including two Cannes Lions and three Effie Awards for work in the Automotive Industry in addition to exclusive Gold and Bronze Effie Awards in Shopper Marketing.

Doug's infectious passion and drive helps inspire his Saatchi & Saatchi X teams to exceed the clients' needs as well his staff's personal expectations. He is a living, breathing personification of the Saatchi & Saatchi X mantra: "Nothing is Impossible."

Doug Van Andel, My Thoughts

I first contacted Doug because of a great Toyota spot he'd just won a Gold Pencil and Lion for. That was back in '2002 and we've been friends and working together ever since.

Doug is the kind of person whose voice always seems to be smiling. And we do a lot of laughing whenever we speak. But the one story that we always do a lot of laughing about is something that happened many years ago.

He was working in L.A. at the time, I'm in New York, and we had never met. Doug and his family were coming for a visit to my city, so we set up a lunch at a favorite French restaurant of mine.

When Doug and his family arrived, the Maitre D' greeted them as only a French Maitre D' can, told them that Mr. Growick would be there shortly, showed them to their table, gave them their menus, then sat down at the table and began to talk to them.

Doug and his wife looked at each other with the "what the hell is this?" kind of look, but were polite. The Maitre D' asked all sorts of bizarre questions and as the entire family incredulously listened, thinking this to be normal for a New York French restaurant Maitre D', his accent began to slowly change from French to American. Or, to be more precise, New Yorkese.

It was me. I couldn't help myself. The devil made me do it.

It took a few seconds for this to sink in with Doug, then he and his family burst out laughing and he almost killed me with his bread knife.

What this tells you about Doug is that:

    A. He is a total gentleman
    B. He has an incredible sense of humor
    C. He is still happily innocent enough to be unfailingly polite
    D. He is, at heart, a Los Angeles tourist
    E. He is vicious with a butter knife in his hand

My First Time
By Doug Van Andel

It was late February of 1989, and I had been part of the creative department of Saatchi & Saatchi/DFS (presently, Saatchi/LA) for only a few weeks. I was hired as their newest art director, without a pre-determined team, defined job, or a designated partner – I was in "creative limbo", a floater, so I went wherever I was sent, just happy to be there.

Prior to joining Saatchi, my career consisted of working behind, what it was called at the time, "The Orange Curtain", basically the pejorative nickname given the comparatively smaller advertising community that resided in Orange County, CA during the mid and late 80's; and a far cry from the "big time" agency life I had fantasized myself in. It was hard to break out from behind the Orange Curtain. Scaling the actual Berlin Wall, which was still in standing at the time, was a far less difficult task. But if you could land a job with a major shop, you actually had a shot.

My first real creative assignment began as a loaner-creative to the "general accounts" group. The group was led by a guy who would eventually become a very good friend, an Associate Creative Director (ACD), but on this day he was a stranger to me and me to him.

I felt he didn't like me much. Why should he? I was an interloper. He was nice enough – an affable sense of humor, a razor-sharp wit, and a masterful storyteller who seemed to keep his team protectively under his wing.

The dynamic of the team was sort of like an exclusive club and it wasn't looking for any new members. They were all fairly young, with stereotypical creative egos, fragile, volatile, and slightly eccentric. The ACD's indifference was soon shared by the rest. I was there, but didn't belong.

What precipitated my being thrust onto the "Young Guns" team was this: a new assignment had come in from Pioneer Electronics, and it was a way to keep me billable while they figured out what to do with me long-term.

We all got briefed in the ACD's office. It didn't seem too complicated to me; as memory serves, the brief stated that they needed to build awareness for Pioneer's retail sales associates training and expertise in the area of customized audio systems for home and vehicle." Here's the rub, the budget had to be $50k or less. A detail that was all but disregarded by my temporary teammates. The feeling was that if the clients saw something they really liked, they'd cough up the cash to produce it, no matter what it might cost. It was a tactic that seemed to have worked for this team and ACD pretty well in the past. Unfortunately, nobody told me so I foolishly stuck dutifully to the brief and thought of ideas that potentially could be produced for the conservative sum of fifty grand without too much difficulty.

The day the team was scheduled to share ideas with the ACD and account leader came and went; but the date never made it to my little isolated cubicle. So I walked over to the ACD's office where he thanked me for the effort but said, they were in good shape and dismissed me...and I do mean dismissed me. I admit it, I was kind of hurt, so I asked, no insisted, at least look at my contribution. If he wanted to dismiss it, that was his prerogative – maybe I'd even learn something.

He graciously pulled the account manager into an impromptu creative review and...they liked it! Ok, more accurately, they didn't hate it.

I called the campaign "Sound Thinking". The idea was to point out that stereo dealers were idiots who tried to sell the most expensive equipment they could with no consideration for what the customer actually needed. The Pioneer Dealer was different, they were trained to give the kind of customized treatment that only die-hard audiophiles enjoyed.

The campaign was supported by a logo "lock-up" I designed with the Pioneer's "Omega" symbol as the "O" in the word SOUND – inspired. Well, at least simple. Other campaign elements consisted of print, POS, outdoor and TV spots. The TV spots featured a cute little jack russell terrier and spokesman, alone on a void set.

My campaign was the only submission that was realistically within the prescribed budget and with the recommendation by the account manager, my campaign was going in front of the client. The other ideas that were bigger and flashier then mine, It appeared "Sound Thinking" didn't have a prayer of selling.

The day after the presentation, the ACD found his way to my cubical to deliver the news in person as to how the meeting went. To my utter surprise and the chagrin of a few, *"Sound Thinking"* had been sold.

Before I knew it, I found myself in a flurry of meetings to discuss the details. A broadcast producer was assigned to me to help with the production, a young woman, a New York transplant, hard-boiled beyond her years. While I had limited television production experience up to that point, I was not a complete production neophyte. I had done a few small spots while still behind the Orange Curtain, This only accentuated the green the broadcast producer saw in me and we started feuding almost immediately – she didn't like me or the color green at all.

Apparently, she didn't realize who I was. I was the hot-shot new-hire whose very first campaign won the shoot-out with the "young guns". Yeah, I was feeling pretty full of myself. I got a fast lesson on the skepticism and distain for flash-in-the-pan up-starts within agency creative departments. By the looks of things, that's exactly what I was, and she did not like it.

The weeks leading up to the actual shoot day, I was introduced to just how political a place an agency can be. This is when I also learned that any production in the ad business requires the coordination and collaboration of a number of skilled cross-functional participants. No place is this more apparent than in the production of a TV campaign.

The morning of the shoot had finally arrived. It was to happen at "The Erector Set", a small sound stage in Hollywood. It's not there anymore, joining the legion of ghosts that have faded into tinsel-town oblivion, but it was Hollywood, where production happened.

By the time I parked, walked five blocks to the stage, the critical decisions had been made without me. Lighting, camera angles, wardrobe all had been locked and were ready to commit to film. My producer had intentionally marginalized my role in my own TV shoot and there simply wasn't anything I could do about it. What made matters worse, the agency's Executive Creative Director had decided to make a rare showing that morning. He, however, was told the correct time and preceded my arrival by nearly an hour. I guess I don't have to tell you, it looked bad for me and the ECD's greeting of "nice of you to join us" didn't help the day or my inaugural campaign get off to a great start.

The glow from the out-of-the-blocks success I had experienced a few weeks prior had long-since faded and now I felt as if I was in real trouble and my future with the agency was questionable.

After the production, things didn't get much better between me and the producer. The post-production phase was riddled with misfortune. A series of simple and cheap TV commercials were quickly becoming an embarrassment and the production a laughing stock at the agency. My ego, self-confidence, and experience were under constant scrutiny by everyone, including myself, and I expected that at any moment, my foray into big-agency life would abruptly and unceremoniously come to an end; like the ignited fumes from a propane tank just before it goes empty. I needed help.

Then something miraculous happened, we finished. What's more, my relationship with the indifferent ACD, warmed and it looked as though I had survived, after all.

Eventually I was placed on the Toyota team where I was paired with a brilliantly talented copywriter partner, to whom I am still very close, and we began a long and very fruitful string of creative successes.

There are a number of things that I learned through this first adventure that I find still hold relevance today:

Number 1: Stick to the brief – sort of. figuratively and/or literally. In other words, what the primary objective is, including budget constraints. It will discipline the creative process. And If you can't "think outside the box", at least make sure it's a really sweet box.

Number 2: Act like a *veteran* not a *victim*. Regardless of your experience level if you act like a victim, you're leaving blood in the water and sharks can smell blood for miles. I allowed myself to think like a victim through the earliest parts of this assignment and it made it easy for my teammates to dismiss me.

Victims are weak and easily paralyzed by doubt. Veterans are rarely phased by little calamity because they trust themselves, and they are nearly always respected, which leads me to the third thing.

Number 3: Respect everyone. Treat everyone with respect, no matter where you fall on the org chart. Even if you don't get it, give it. Respect is the most valuable free currency you have and can spread in all directions, patch a lot of misunderstandings and sooth a lot of bruised egos. My conflicts with that broadcast producer might have been greatly improved had I chose to trust and respect her more than even she did me, no matter how it assaulted my ego.

Number 4: Stay ravenously curious about what makes people tick. Human nature is one of the most consistent and underestimated forces in the universe. It never gets dull and the understanding becomes extremely useful at doing what we do.

Finally, Number 5: There may be no "I" in "team", but there is in CLIO and after that happened, that's what the *"Sound Thinking"* campaign finally won in the category of small budget retail campaigns. I simply wouldn't have survived without help from dedicated and talented team, especially a curtain broadcast producer from NYC, kicking my ass.

At the risk of slipping one last pun into this anecdote, It's comforting to know that sound thinking really does prevail in the end.

While it looks extremely dated, and the resolution is not so great, here's the link to only surviving cut I still have. Enjoy:

https://secure.vimeo.com/40835384

Yacco Vijn
Creative Managing Director, TBWA\Amsterdam

Yacco Vijn is an award-winning digital creative director with 15 years experience in both integrated + interactive marketing & advertising.

Before joining TBWA\NEBOKO Amsterdam as Managing Creative Director Yacco co-founded digital agency KONG which in 2010 was the only dutch agency to be listed in the Cannes Lions hotlist of international independent agencies and highest ranked dutch agency in Promo + Activation. Prior to KONG Yacco worked as a creative director at POKE in London, was co-founder at interactive agency Skipintro, associate creative director at Lowe Digital and a globetrotting techno DJ. He's worked with global brands such as AXE, Orange, Orangina Schweppes International, Mercedes-Benz, Ministry of Justice, Samsung Mobile and others. He's won many awards including at Cannes Lions, Art Directors Club and Webbys to name but a few and has also been juror at the Cannes Cyber Lions, Webbys, FWA and Art Directors Club.

Yacco's work has been featured in The New York Times, on Apple.com, The Guardian, in books such as 'Convergence Media History' and on events like FlashForward in New York. He's done workshops for Dove marketeers in Germany, Hyper Island students in Sweden, Hylink creatives in Beijing and Shanghai and at PANL and Adobe XL in Amsterdam.

Yacco Vijn, My Thoughts

Until he recently became the Managing Creative Director at TBWA/Amsterdam, Yacco had been the founder and CCO of KONG/Amsterdam, a top digital shop, and had been a Cannes Digital Judge last year.

Oddly enough, I got to know Yacco because he had done his homework most diligently, believed he could trust me to find some top talent for him in the States; and he wanted to get to find out more about me and for me to find out about him.

So what did I find out? Yacco has one of the most generous and infectious laughs; the kind that makes you laugh along even if you hadn't expected to.

He's passionate about the work he does, the work his people do under his tutelage, and passionate about the proper creative solutions for his clients.

He's eager and quick to praise his colleagues in Amsterdam and those he admires worldwide; and funny, but his opinions usually dovetail with mine rather nicely. Which makes it easier to laugh some more.

Yacco is like one of those Old World craftsmen, who we in the States seem to picture hunched over an ancient worktable, cobbling together magical shoes, or wondrous watches, with his elves waiting patiently for the masterpiece to be finished and presented with a smile and a masterful flourish.

And you know what, that's not too far from exactly what he does.

My First Time
By Yacco Vijn

Flashback 1998: Sir Frank Lowe had just acquired Kuiper & Schouten, the most awarded dutch agency in The Netherlands and stuck LOWE in front of the agency's name. The partners at LK&S had gone their ways and one of the former partners - Hans van Dijk, who happened to be the most awarded Dutch copywriter of all time - had eventually returned to set up Lowe Digital, a (you guessed it) digitally focused sister (or brother) of the traditional agency LK&S. Lowe Digital was conveniently located near the Vondelpark in Amsterdam and from the moment I walked into the office I knew I would do some good work there.

At Lowe Digital I was quite fortunate to be working with Hans, who taught me everything there is to know about the advertising business in turboboost. We did a lot of solid web-work at Lowe Digital for financials, telecoms, food, non-food and those ever Fast Moving Consumer Goods. I was promoted from jr. Art Director to Art Director to Associate Creative Director to Creative Partner (which I rejected since I wasn't interested in the whole partnership thing) in a little under a year until a merger came along that made the whole agency go to shambles. Good thing I didn't become a partner there after all.

Apart from working hard and building the agency's rep we also had a lot of fun. What came out of these moments of having fun and fooling around was registering the domain name 'Skipintro.com' for which we made a really long intro which we stuck on the domain. It was a parody on the thing that was all the rage at the time: Flash Intros and the Skip Intro button that came along with them. The intro consisted of all the cliches that we knew from the likes of Gabocorp; bouncing balls, pretentious copy and in-your-face music and sound effects. The parody was a bit of a succes, it slotted over 13 million unique visits within a year and got picked up by the New York Times in the US, The Guardian and Times in the UK and all Dutch newspapers that mattered. Kevin Lynch, the CCO of Macromedia at the time, used Skipintro in his Flashback 2000 keynote in New York during the FlashForward 2000 festival where he showcased everything that was important to the 'rise of Flash'. And even just a few years ago I got an email asking if it was OK to include Skipintro.com in a book called 'Convergence Media History'.

There wasn't any premium travelling to exotic locations, no fancy photographers or hip directors involved in the Skipintro.com 'project' - just us having a few late nights of foolish fun. What Skipintro made us realise was that on the web, it was all about stuff worth sharing and that if you created something that people found worth sharing, it could go crazy. From that moment on we tried to bend our commercial work in such a way that we thought it would be worth sharing. The cheeky project that was Skipintro.com gave us direction in what we believed worked on the web not only for advertising but for everything else too.

And so after a disastrous merger between Lowe and Lintas (everything Lintas did eventually ended in tears – Jon Hegarty even wrote about it in his book 'Hegarty on Advertising') we left the agency and decided to start our own agency: Skipintro, where we did a lot of award-winning work that resonated beyond the advertising space and that people found worth sharing for clients like The Rijksmuseum.

Years later, in 2007 when I had a stint as Creative Director at an agency called Poke in London I can remember going out for a dinner with a bunch of Pokers and one of the guys there mentioning Skipintro – 'that was epic - that must have been the first ever Viral!'. Which reminded me again that the work we probably made in our most foolish moment still mattered to a few people so many years later.

I guess it's a little like Steve Jobs said: Stay Foolish.

Nancy Vonk
Co-founder of Swim

Nancy Vonk was Co-Chief Creative Officer of Ogilvy Toronto before founding a creative leadership training lab, Swim, with long-time partner Janet Kestin in 2011.

They have won many top industry awards including Cannes Lions, One Show Pencils and Clios. They are the creative directors of Dove "Evolution", winner of two Grand Prix at Cannes, and "Diamond Shreddies, winner of a Grand Clio.

Nancy has judged many of the world's top advertising awards shows including Cannes, Clios, One Show and D&AD. In '08 she was the first female chair in the history of the Art Director's Club of New York.

Nancy and Janet's honors include being named to Creativity magazine's Top 50 creative people of '08, advertising Women of the Year at the WIN Awards in LA and the AWNY Awards in NY in '07, and induction into Canada's Marketing Hall of Legends in '11. They have a widely read advice column, "Ask Jancy" on ad site ihaveanidea.org. They penned a critically acclaimed Adweek book, "Pick Me", in 2005. It has become a staple in advertising schools from Texas to Turkey. They are currently writing a business book for HarperCollins.

Nancy is a mentor and frequent lecturer at ad schools including the renowned VCU Brandcenter. She has been on the board of the One Club since '09.

Nacny Vonk, My Thoughts

OK. This is an interesting one.

Though I've only spoken to Nancy a few times, and have been in communication with her via email only a few more times than that, I felt that I knew her years before we were ever in contact.

Cue Twilight Zone music. No, no, cut the music.

This had nothing to do with ESP, or ESPN, or any of that. It had to do with her creative partner of twenty years, Janet Kestin, of whom you already know (if you've been reading in alphabetic order). Janet had filled me in in spades. Hearts, really, but who's counting?

But if you haven't been reading in alphabetical order, no problem. Here's the skinny on Nancy. You saw that glamour "Whos behind the Foster Grants?" photo. That smile says everything.

Nancy is as warm as toast, but not crusty. Forgetting the creative part, which is a a given or she never would've gotten where she is, whenever I've mentioned Nancy to anyone in the creative world, they break into a giant smile. Even on the phone, you can feel the smile. She's just that kind of person.

You get a sugar rush just listening to people talk about her.

In my introduction, I talked about those who mentor and menace. Trust me, Nancy is Ms. Mentor. In spades.

Hearts, really.

My First Time

By Nancy Vonk

Our family lore has it that before I could talk, I would often stand in front of the bathroom mirror holding a bottle of dish liquid and babble in tones recognizable from the TV commercials of the day. I was holding something VERY SPECIAL up to that glass. My big fake smile, wide eyes and animated body language made that clear. So technically, I cranked out my first ad around age 2.

I became that kid who was drawing constantly, always the best artist in class. By 7ish I vividly remember drawing a sort of storyboard for an Ivory soap commercial. I was inspired by the tiny silver bubbles that radiated from the bar when I held it under a blast of water in the tub. I wanted everyone to know how amazing this was, and television was the obvious place to reach my target of everyone. (No savant, strategic thinking wouldn't show up until a couple of decades later.)

Now, you would think a career in advertising or some other creative field might naturally unfold with this kind of foreshadowing. But I was well into my university years before I stopped balking at channeling my creative talents into a living. I thought that would wreck everything. Art was supposed to be fun, not a job. It eventually dawned on me that using what you're reasonably good at is how it works. I had numerous summer jobs to underscore my incompetence at anything related to math or physical labor.

I had report cards filled with evidence I should really narrow things down to either art or writing. One English prof strongly advised against a job in journalism when I showed interest. (She was a bitter, former journalist.) I stumbled into "graphic communications" at the University of Delaware after attending a dynamic presentation about the program given by the young head of the department, Ray Nichols. As I considered a major in art history, art education, fine arts and photography, suddenly advertising jumped out. "That looks like fun" is about as deep and complex as the thought process went as I chose my path.

The program was very intense; our class of 60 dropped to 12 by the time I graduated. I left school with a good portfolio and a lot of experience with all-nighters and high stress. I was first in my major, and felt pretty well prepared for the "real world", but in short order I was thrown by how protracted the job search proved to be. After about 14 interviews in the D.C. area I was feeling desperate. (Genius reason to look there? Home of my two best friends.) I was on the all-Cheerios, all-the-time diet and was willing to work for a printing house with an opening for a "paste-up" artist at this point. I had the first big break of my career: the kindly owner said he'd be happy to hire me, but advised I should keep looking for what I went to school to accomplish. The very next interview was in posh Georgetown, at a tiny shop of maybe 17 people. Bingo. I was a junior art director.

I didn't have that first job people like Sally Hogshead and Ted Royer can look back on loaded with global awards, stellar accounts and high profile creative leaders. While little Sal and Ted were at the pode accepting hardware, I was designing menus and hotel brochures. I was doing mechanicals, changing the chemicals in the dark room, and making some minor contribution to the creative director's ads on occasion. I was so excited to see "my" ad in Time magazine (a redesign of an existing ad done by someone else). To think my parents would add that very issue to their giant stack of Time's in the basement closet---amazing.

Designing a program for a Lena Horne concert was another thrill. (Photo provided, no shoot or actual contact with the diva.) We often worked with talented photographers and illustrators; the awards I recall were craft awards for their work. I got to shoot with Bret Littlehales and was so impressed he shot for National Geographic, as his father had before him.

Looking back, I was in exactly the right place for me. It wasn't my first, second or 13th choice. At this tiny shop I got a view to the way the whole agency worked. I got to make lots of mistakes without penalty. I learned about teamwork. I learned from wonderful people including an absolute wild woman, Sam Macuga, the creative director. I emulated her bold style and fearlessness (though I had to fake that for a good while). Gender was a non-event, to watch her in action. It didn't occur to me for a very long time that some women have a hard go based on gender.

I went up the ladder slowly, but surely. In my first job I had no ambition but to not be fired. I was painfully insecure and part of my successful journey was thanks to others believing in me. I was bossy as all get-out since birth, but it wasn't on my to-do list to lead and in fact I had to be pushed to take bigger and bigger titles over the years.

I think everything happens for a reason, and timing is everything. Things worked out, in spite of my first ad being so inconsequential, I can't remember it. (Unless you count the age-7 Ivory commercial, which to be fair, wasn't produced.)

Your first job doesn't have to be at Crispin or R/GA or Droga5. You will learn valuable lessons anywhere. If you don't shoot to the ad stratosphere in record time, or any time soon, fret not. By all means, knock on the doors where you'd kill to work. But when those very few dream openings go to others, believe me, there is reason to go on living.

Steve Vranakis
Creative Director, EMEA, Google Creative Lab

Steve brings almost 20 years of experience to Google from the world of digital, design and advertising. Some of the campaigns he's most recently been involved with include: the launch of Google+ 'A life lived and shared', the 'Jamal Edwards' Chrome better web campaign, the Vs. g+ debates series featuring Richard Branson and Russell Brand and the YouTube Space Lab Channel and launch video. Steve has worked at some of the biggest and best creative agencies in the world including: VCCP London, Foote Cone & Belding San Francisco, WCRS Arnold Worldwide Partners in London, Modem Media UK and DDB in his native Vancouver.

Steve was named the number 1 New Media Creative in Campaign's "10 Hottest Digital Creatives of 2000 and 2009" as well as making their 'A List' in 2003, 2008 - 2010. In 2005, Steve made Campaign magazine's 'Top 15 digital creatives list and Revolution's 50 Power List in 2007. In 2008 he made their top ten. His industry accolades include his work on BMW as the first ever 'e-ad' to be chosen as Campaign Magazine's "Pick of the Week", and also the best interactive ad of the year along with his work being recognised by the D&AD, One Show's, Campaign Big Awards, BTA's, Clio's, Cannes Lions, the Casies, SF Show, Adweek's MC Icon, Revolution, New Media Age, London International Advertising, the Andy Awards, the Reggies and the Lotus Awards. Steve was also a key part of the hugely successful Comparethemeerkat.com that is sited as one of the most successful social media campaigns ever. Both the Book and iPhone app that were created for Comparethemeerkat.com have gone straight to number one.

Steve Vranakis, My Thoughts

Steve must have been a canine in a former life. Not that he's a dog, he's just such a great friend.

When I first started bothering Steve, his wife was in Greece having a baby, he was wondering about the future, and we had long talks about what he should be doing and where.

As it turned out, he could do anything and anywhere.

Steve is the type of person who will do everything in his power to create the right solution to a client's problem, while at the same time creating an atmosphere of creative collegiality for those on his team.

Steve just likes people. And they like him.

Steve also gets so excited about ideas and events. We met for breakfast in New York right before SXSW and he was just so psyched about GOOGLE. And though he couldn't speak about anything specific, he spoke in glowing vowels and syllables about what they were doing, what they could do, what they were going to do. I sat there fascinated then ran out and bought a big block of stock. Just on his vowels and syllables.

Steve also invited put me in touch with friends in London who he thought might be important in moving MFT along and he was absolutely right. He always does nice things like that.

I actually saw Steve help a little old lady across the street. Really. Of course she didn't want to go across the street, but that did not deter Steve from escorting her there anyway. I'm not sure if she ever got back.

My First Time
By Steve Vranakis

What did we do before the Internet?

In 1993 I was a young graphic designer who'd just sublet a small studio space in one of Vancouver's 'up and coming' areas. Like many designers just starting out, my main clients included club promoters, DJ's, photographers and this wacky lot who were going to bring the Internet to Canada…

The two Dave's just walked in one day and asked if I knew anything about the 'information superhighway' and if I was keen to help them launch an ISP, one of Canada's first. At that time the Internet was in its infancy, at least in Canada. And although I answered that I was very familiar with it and what an Internet service provider was, I was totally making it up…

Don't get me wrong, I had played around on a few BBS' a bit but believe it or not browsers didn't really exist. E-mail was just being born and only accessible through plonky client software and even web sites were few and far between.

I was in a bit of a bind, I needed to find out everything I could and fast about the Internet but there was no way of getting on-line yet! How's that for a paradox.

No real search, no Wiki, just a really slow US Robotics 2400 baud modem I had borrowed from a service bureau and a copy of NCSA Mosaic that I got free as a floppy disk on the inside cover of an O'Reilly book about the 'World Wide Web.'

The two Dave's quickly realized that I had no idea what they were talking about but liked my work and thought I could be useful to them in helping them launch their company and brand. (I also got them into loads of clubs as I kept many of the flyers and VIP passes I was designing at the time) They spoke to me about how they wanted to launch this thing across the country, pile on the subscribers and ultimately take the company public. All of which they did with their newly appointed 22 year old creative dude who still had no idea what they were talking about.

I remember when I finally did get on-line. I was on a pre-Power PC Mac and everything was installed via floppy. I still remember the screech of the modem, the on screen animation plotting its progress, the blinking of the LEDS and the constant dropping of my connection!!! I wasn't impressed.

But after about half a dozen reboots of the modem, I finally got on-line.

I remember my disbelief that I was connected to countless other people (probably about 7) from all over the world from my second hand Mac in Gas town, Vancouver. It was pretty incredible. Just me and this screen staring back at me, telling me like a Manhattan members' club doorman, 'you're in'. You made it.

That was the easy bit. Now all I had to do was figure this thing out and its appeal, how to position it, who would want it and why. The good thing was that the Internet just kind of sold itself. The notion of connecting to countless people and content all over the world was a bit of a no brainer.

I just had to make a national print and outdoor campaign, design the software packaging and website in a matter of months along with countless trade show booths and even an infomercial... not one of my finest moments.

The campaign was more 'Klingon' in look and feel than really creative but it got the message across and they signed up in droves despite it being my first true large scale launch.

I've since been part of many high profile global launches but for products and services that have been around for a while for the most part.

We became the biggest, went national and eventually floated. I was lucky enough to get in on the IPO, which bought me a 1963 Pontiac Acadian convertible. Silver with Red interior. It eventually succumbed to the rust that was plaguing its undercarriage and it died a slow and expensive death.

But boy was it a fun ride.
I stuck with that internet thing and went on to have a bit of a love affair with it even becoming a bit of an expert at the time which had the big agency

networks continuously courting me to come in-house and be their digital dude which I eventually did for quite a few.

I learnt a hell of a lot a in a very short space of time and how important it was to really understand whatever it was that you were attempting to communicate (even if it didn't exist yet) and truly get under its skin. I figured out pretty quickly that people didn't want to buy the technology bit but more how it made their lives that much better. There was no point in trying to explain packet switching to them when all they wanted to do was surf the corners of the globe for hours on end.

It's weird to have been involved with something that went on to start a communications revolution. The Internet's been good to me and I'm happy to have met it so early in my career, even if at first I had no idea what it was.

Phil Growick

Phil is the Managing Director of the Howard-Sloan-Koller Group in New York City, the retained executive search firm specializing in top talent in all forms of media.

His friendships with some of the world's most influential advertising creatives led to this book's creation.

New editions in the My First Time series to be published shortly are:

MFT W: Top Women Creatives In The World
MFT, Jr.: Top Junior World Creatives
MFT2

Phil's first Sherlock Holmes novel, The Secret Journal of Dr. Watson, was published this May. A sequel is in the works. At that time, all the questions left unanswered, will be.

Lightning Source UK Ltd.
Milton Keynes UK
UKOW030151070912

198586UK00005B/93/P